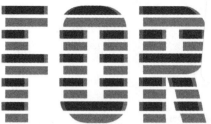

FOR

HEALTH

HORIZONS OF CARE BEYOND AUSTERITY

AUTON-

REFLECTIONS FROM GREECE

OMY

CARENOTES COLLECTIVE

FOR HEALTH AUTONOMY

HORIZONS OF CARE BEYOND AUSTERITY
REFLECTIONS FROM GREECE

CARENOTES COLLECTIVE

For Health Autonomy: Horizons of Care Beyond Austerity—Reflections from Greece
CareNotes: A Notebook of Health Autonomy
CareNotes Collective (editors)

ISBN: 978-1-942173-14-4
LCCN: 2019946829
10 9 8 7 6 5 4 3 2 1

CareNotes, carenotes@protonmail.com
https://www.commonnotions.org/carenotes

Common Notions
c/o Interference Archive
314 7th Street
Brooklyn, NY 11215

Common Notions
c/o Making Worlds Bookstore
210 S. 45th Street
Philadelphia, PA 19104

www.commonnotions.org
info@commonnotions.org

Cover design by Josh MacPhee / Antumbra Design
Layout design and typesetting by Morgan Buck / Antumbra Design
Antumbra Design www.antumbradesign.org

Printed in the USA on acid-free, recycled paper

CONTENTS

THE COMMON IS US
PRINCIPLES OF HEALTH AUTONOMY

Silvia Federici

What does it mean to recreate notions of the common around health, especially in light of today's situations? To start with a small example from everyday life before moving onto more general themes, let me describe a common scene. I go to the park near where I live every morning. One recent morning there was a big run for ovarian cancer where there were several hundred people gathered wearing blue shirts. You may imagine another moment, perhaps pink shirts for breast cancer. I understand from what I read about these nonprofit organizations that very little, at best 5 percent, of the money gathered actually goes to research. Instead, the money goes into the coffers of the organizations hosting these marches. Meanwhile, many participate enthusiastically, run, go home, and feel like they've done their work. Yet despite the advancement of great medical industries, people are getting sicker than ever. Our bodies and our minds are deteriorating. Is there an alternative to accepting a life of misery in which social and economic impoverishment leads to the impoverishment of one's health?

It seems to me that there are many alternatives or possibilities that can come to mind. Let's, for instance, put this scene in the frame of an old and significant short book called *Witches, Midwives, and Healers: A History of Women Healers*, written by Barbara Ehrenreich and Deirdre English in 1973 (recently republished in a second edition by the Feminist Press). It was this publication that inspired me to write *The Caliban and the Witch*. I am reminded of a very interesting section about a popular health movement that took place in the United States in the 1830s that renounced doctors as an elite group that didn't care for the wellbeing of the people. At the time, medicine was very rudimentary, mostly involving techniques of bloodletting as treatment for whatever diseases patients may have. The slogan of this popular movement was "every person a doctor." Various communities formed groups, and women formed "ladies physiology counsels" across the country to study the body and to figure out forms of illness prevention. They were much more focused on prevention than on treatment—the idea animating this movement was a reclamation of control of their bodies and a reclamation of essential knowledge of their bodies. We see in their organizing the expectation that these kinds of knowledge cannot only come from above but rather must come from below. Indeed, all across the country, people came together to discuss what it means to be well. What is health? What is it that we know? And what is it that we can share?

This history offers a very simple but powerful example of the difference between a statist or market relation to health—in which health providers are organized in the form of institutions and health services are delivered from above—and a conception of health that is a movement built from below. This distinction was very important then and remains so in our time of manifold and compounding crises. Health autonomy is central to the many mobilizations I believe we must engage in. Even though we don't currently have control of many of the means that are necessary to replace the power of existing institutions, we can nevertheless begin to do things in our everyday lives to start reclaiming control. That, in essence, is the principle of the common.

The common, quite simply, is a particular way of organizing society. It is a particular way of conceiving relations among people and also relations to the means of production, relations to the land, relations to natural abundance, and to the wealth that we produce. The common is reflected in a very classic conception of what communalism is supposed to stand for. It means a society where we have access to natural wealth, the wealth we produce, cooperation, and government from below. These being very general concepts, the challenge arises of how we realize it. How do we realize it in a society where so much has been taken away from us? The robbery, the expropriation, the dispossession that forms the basis of capitalism is continuous and ongoing. Indeed, in nearly all parts of the world, we are witnessing a major expansion of capitalist relations and major forms of dispossession.

In this context, it is all the more crucial that we do not mislead ourselves into living life as separate individuals. It is a principle of the common, that the common is us, and if other people get sick, we get sick. The principle of being responsible for the life of others is really fundamental. As the Movement for Black Lives reminds us, "none of us are free until all of us are free."

Asserting the principle of the common is more important than ever as we are witnessing a major assault on all of the earth and social commons. As the Amazon burns and as new mines in disparate parts of the planet force the displacement of entire populations from their ancestral lands, we see the degree of the destruction that is taking place in our lifetimes. Of course, it's not only in terms of land; it's also in terms of the urban spaces in which so many of us live.

The question then is: how do we recuperate our collective capacity to make decisions about our lives? That is, how we do not only recuperate communal relations to land, but recuperate control over what we eat and the kind of life we live? How do we recuperate control over the water we drink in urban spaces, the air we breathe? This is an issue that has to be at the center of every struggle because our struggles cannot only be oppositional, they must also be constructive and create the seeds of the society in which we want to live. This means that an element of communalism has to be built into every struggle.

Much of my own work in the last decade and longer has been critical of the conception of 'the common' often assumed in radical milieus—for instance, a conception based on the digital commons, on the internet, and generally on the use of digital technology. I'm not suggesting that we do not use these forms of communication, but there are important limits to what they provide. Digital commons are problematic because to produce digital technology requires immense destruction of, and extraction from, land and waters around the planet. A society that is centered on digital commons will demand that we continue to expropriate people from their land, as is happening today in so many parts of Africa and Latin America. This is a real problem that we have to confront.

If we speak of building a society on the principle of self-government and sharing, then that society has to be organized in a way that reproduces our life. It means that a struggle for the common has to include a struggle about land, about food, about water, and at its center, about health. Those struggles are fundamental because we cannot have a new society that is not capable of reproducing itself. Reproducing ourselves implies collectively restoring the land and waters of this planet to communal use against historic and ongoing colonial and capitalist enclosures. This does not mean that every person has to make a struggle around that, but it means that there has to be a wider movement that includes these struggles.

When I began to be interested in the question of the common, all my sympathy and interest went to people who were already in the eighties organizing around the issue of land or, like Vandana Shiva, were defending the forests. However, I have been particularly interested also in the question of how we communalize the reproduction of every everyday life in terms of the actual activities by which life is reproduced, not only housework or domestic work, but reproductive work in general—including child raising, health care, education, and the production and circulation of knowledge. This is the great terrain that sustains our life, it is also a terrain of struggle because all these activities are constantly being appropriated by the capitalist class and put at the service of capitalist production, of the labor market, and of the consumer economy. Indeed, all of these activities are already battlefields, while also fostering the conditions for communal forms of reproduction. The commoning of reproductive activities, at all levels, is very important to guarantee survival and to not depend completely on the market and the state for our reproduction.

It remains a crucial question how all of these struggles and initiatives may connect with each other. What is the common ground? Clearly each of us or each community is capable of fighting around certain issues. But we can't each fight against the whole spectrum of theft and violence that upholds this current society. What is important is that we connect with other people so that our struggles do not remain isolated. Breaking down the isolation in which we live is fundamental, not only to guarantee our survival, but also to confront the state with more power and continue our struggle in the longer term.

When we look at the experience of working people's struggles, anarchist or non-anarchist struggles of all types in the history of the labor movement of the United States, the same pattern emerges whenever a strike takes on a revolutionary dimension. I speak of those moments when the strike goes beyond the union pattern, when people know that this is it, that they are going not to back down. At that moment, the way people reproduce their day to day life shifts. In other words, people don't just meet on the picket line, but rather through the whole spectrum of their reproduction—they share food, exchange services, and share all the resources they have. It's only with the solidarity that comes from commoning that we build the capacity to confront the police, the bosses, and the state.

I have also been very inspired by the experience of Latin America where communal relations are still strong, in great part because of the presence of Indigenous people's movement that have maintained communal forms of life. Moreover, at a time of great economic and social crisis, people across the continent, particularly women, have responded to displacement, to dispossessions, and repeated austerity programs by organizing communal ways of reproducing everyday life, whether it be with collective kitchens or urban gardens or cooperative childcare. And it is not only Latin America. Many of the same initiatives have been happening in other places, though they may not have achieved the same degree of connectivity. This is one of the things that we have to build. All of this rests on transforming the way we relate to each other, the way we live, our ability to break down isolation.

Another fundamental issue is temporality. We must think about struggle in the long term—the temporal dimensions of our movement's direction. Where are we going to go? What are our ultimate goals? As soon as we take a more long-term approach, we realize that we cannot achieve it unless we have a particular type of reproductive infrastructure.

Reclaiming our collective memory, the memory of struggles that were fought in the places where we live and act, is particularly important. Communities that have a stronger sense of their history— a stronger sense of where they come from, of the battles that have been fought, of the history of the ground on which they fight, or of the community in which they live—are able to create a deeper sense of connection among people, a collective subject, and a sense of a common interest. These communities are better able to resist when a mining company comes to town than those in which everybody is individualized or separated. This is why in the United States and elsewhere so much institutional planning and energy goes into destroying that memory. (If there is an important monument in the history of people's struggles, you can be sure they will destroy it; if there is an African or Indigenous burial ground, they will pave over it and build real estate on top of it, or run a pipeline through it.)

In reclaiming memory we are also affirming another principle of the common, which is that our solidarity should not only go to the living, but also to our dead. When we talk about commoning, it should also be for the dead. The history of the atrocities that have been committed, in the form of slavery or the genocide of Indigenous peoples or of the witch hunts against women, have to be a living presence in our struggles. In so many dispossessed communities it is already there, as is the case with communities in Latin America who have ingrained the memory of the dead and disappeared into their struggles. Rituals of resistance such as some of the celebrations that take place during the Day of the Dead are significant. Raising the awareness of the injustices that were committed, bringing back the memory of those who were killed and those who fought, places our struggles in a longer history and this makes it stronger. It is also a way of not allowing those crimes to be forgotten and to go unpunished. When thinking of the future, we must keep in mind those who have come before us. As so many women have told me, particularly in Guatemala where so many have been killed, it's that kind of capacity to make the dead living that gives communities the courage to confront forces that seem far superior to ours. It gives us the courage to understand that our immediate struggles to improve our lives are part of a much longer and powerful struggle for liberation.

Brooklyn, NY
September 2019

This text is adapted from a talk delivered
at the 2019 New York Anarchist Book Fair.

THE AUTONOMY OF CARE:
FROM HEALTHCARE TO CARE WORK IN GREECE

CareNotes Collective

> *"At the current situation of intensified deregulation of our lives, as in recent years, the Solidarity Clinics have been a social safety net. The only one in such a broad scale. And this is a fact which cannot be appropriated by any government, party or official institutional body. The fact that we continue to operate has nothing to do with an expectation to get things done as it was before. **We have nowhere to return to. And this is a conscious choice.** In any situation of political and social instability we know that today we have the social relationships and the necessary experience to maintain an active role in social developments."*

—Invitation by Social Solidarity Health Clinics of Athens, Thessaloniki, and Crete to George Caffentzis, 2015

Since the 2008 global crisis, austerity has been a tool widely used by governments in order to discipline certain strata of society and redirect money from the public sector into the private one in times of perceived economic downturn. Greece has been at the center of this global capitalist restructuring, not only suffering from excessive austerity measures, but also continuously assaulted by violence from the state and fascist ideologies. These forces have consequently destroyed services that provide basic necessities such as housing, food, and healthcare. In turn, autonomous collectives and networks based in working-class and migrant communities addressing a range of medical and emotional care needs have been essential in the formation of social clinics, pharmacies, small-scale farms, and soup kitchens. These self-made, remedial institutions have provided migrant support and service exchanges, coordinated the distribution of clothing and foodstuffs, and have trained self-defense committees that protect neighborhoods from armed mafia, police, and fascist organizations such as Golden Dawn.

For Health Autonomy is dedicated to these Greek autonomous care spaces, including all clinics, social spaces for health, social kitchens, and safe spaces liberated from the state and capital. These spaces have reclaimed care beyond the limits of the biomedical, nonprofit, and capitalist frameworks. CareNotes Collective invited friends to share their experiences so that they may inform similar projects elsewhere. We were particularly interested in self-organized care spaces and what is involved in setting up and operating such spaces within the context of austerity. Among the questions raised in the following texts are:

1.   What are the theories or conceptual frameworks guiding autonomous self-organized care practices?

2.   What efforts are made to engage participants in a horizontal process rather than the existing "savior" and "expert" biomedical dynamic?

3.   How do these care work practices deal with the costs associated with securing space, supplies, and wages?

4.   How do collectives engage with other social and political groups, their neighborhoods, and public space in general?

5.   What role, if any, does a broader network of care spaces have in sharing knowledge and other practices against capitalist/ state violence?

The struggles and significance of these spaces intensify at the very moment the state, capital, and complicit institutions attempt to diminish their power via austerity and manufactured crises. While riot police and government bulldozers attack squats, NGOs, evangelical missionaries, drug dealers, and pimps parasitically prey upon migrants and other victims of austerity. Our contributors elaborate on what constitutes autonomous care work in Greece and how these projects may inspire similar possibilities elsewhere. Readers will discover how recent experiences of autonomous care spaces in Greece are central to expanding global anticapitalist struggles around care reproduction and communization.

Beyond the Institutional Narratives of Care

There are over thirty social clinics in Greece. These spaces provide primary and specialized care for roughly ten percent of the population and a rising number of migrants. They operate beyond the financial flows and authority of the state, religious charities, and other external funders. Despite worsening austerity measures and police and fascist violence, these spaces maintain horizontal assemblies that coordinate all aspects of fundraising, medical supplies, care delivery, and emotional support.

Most accounts from academics, journalists, and even some activists only consider Greek autonomous care work in its proximity to modern medicine and reflect upon healthcare reform based on these experiences. Some perceive these spaces as temporary materializations that address only a limited range of health issues by and for activists that disappear once the state and its neoliberal apparatus formulate new healthcare policies or more "efficient" forms of healthcare services. However, such notions rely on a nostalgic misperception of the permanence of a stable and benevolent social welfare state that ensures access to quality healthcare despite decades of neoliberal policies devaluing care workers, closing healthcare facilities, and piling debt upon allied health students. For instance, when tracing the course of the UK's National Health Service or the Affordable Care Act in the US, we can see how care workers are constantly struggling against hospital closures despite increased need by patients, longer work hours, more dangerous labor conditions due to higher patient turnover, and the hidden epidemic of depression, substance use, and suicide gripping care workers and allied health students. The devaluation of care work more broadly is situated within a neoliberal logic that has led to *more* people becoming dependent on healthcare, not less. The biomedical model is falling short of sustaining our well-being while destroying our capacity to collectivize and confront against the violence committed against our bodies and ecologies.

Some doctors, rooted within the biomedical model, may dismiss these social clinics due to their inability to address the more acute dimensions of clinical medicine, such as gunshot wounds, traumatic injuries, or cancer. These require the kind of expert and resource-intensive services that western medicine rests its superiority upon. However, the overwhelming majority of healthcare needs can be addressed using preventative and primary care approaches that market-driven health systems do not deliver evenly or effectively to society.

To fully understand how Greek autonomous care work functions, one must imagine how it operates beyond the biomedical experience. Here, the treatment of pathologies—such as cancers or viruses—is considered as important as dismantling the causes of pathologies, including the social problems of debt, homelessness, police violence, and isolation. We must grasp how the de-individualization of care, what we might refer to as *the communization of care*, is central to fighting state and capital's racialized and gendered forms of abandonment.

Ensuring access to medicine and healthcare is as relevant as liberating unused spaces for housing or de-policing neighborhoods. In chapter eight, "Solidarity Beyond Psychiatry," the Hellenic Observatory for Rights in the Field of Mental Health, for instance, reflects on their experience of launching a public information office within a state-run psychiatric hospital. The office provides advocacy and support for patients and their relatives seeking to access care for emotional suffering, obtain information about treatment, and alternatives to pharmacotherapy. The occupation of the Healthcare

Center of Zagliveri by healthcare workers and community members offers another approach to expanding access to existing healthcare services through worker and patient assemblies (see chapter three, "Details About the End of the World").

To truly grasp the Greek contribution to autonomous care work, one must also understand how the broader autonomous or anticapitalist milieu impacts other modes of noncapitalist life around art, food, housing, or migrant solidarity.

This is not unlike other autonomous currents that have shaped alternative networks, such as the Free Women of Spain during the anarchist movement in 1930s Spain; the hospital occupations and autonomous care work of Black Panthers and Young Lords in 1960s New York City; the clinics and schools of the Landless Workers Movement in Brazil in the 1980s or the Zapatistas since 1994 in Mexico; the barricades of the Oaxaca Commune in 2006 which challenged the gendered nature of social reproduction with collective kitchens and resource distributions; and so many other autonomous currents that have shaped alternative networks, such as Food Not Bombs or community gardens with food sharing, housing through squatting or cooperative living arrangements, and other forms of social reproduction.[1] The contemporary Greek experiments in autonomous life detailed in this book offer an important and all-too-rare glimpse of how struggles today against the state, capital, and the

---

1   See M.E. O'Brien, "Junkie Communism," *Commune.* No. 3, Summer 2019; Barucha Peller, "Self-Reproduction and the Oaxaca Commune," *ROAR,* Spring 2016; Mariarosa Dalla Costa, *Family, Welfare, and the State: From Progessivism to the New Deal* (Brooklyn, NY: Common Notions, 2015); Silvia Federici, *Revolution at Point Zero: Housework, Reproduction, and Feminist Struggle* (Oakland, CA and Brooklyn, NY: PM Press/Common Notions, 2012).

biomedical model simultaneously allow us to locate a revolutionary starting point in care work—where desires for a symbiosis between ourselves and our ecologies are liberated from institutional medicine via collective healing and knowledge-sharing practices.

Autonomous Care

In Greece, this desire for autonomous care spaces is in opposition to capitalist narratives of care, including those financially lucrative modes of "self-care", such as one's *personal* trainer, *my* diet plan, *your* sick leave, that deny possibilities of nurturing mutual aid or socialization around distress and precarity. Much of the self-care industry is produced at the expense of nurses, technicians, and masseuses who are predominantly women of color. In the same way, traditions of the Global South—such as yoga, ayahuasca, and herbal remedies—are robbed of their important contextual relations with the earth, humanity, and spirituality.

The perpetual and intensifying exploitation of working bodies and raw materials for profit are integral to capitalist life. Capitalist-driven "crises" through unemployment, de-industrialization, sexual violence, war, and other strategies have created bodies excluded from flows of capital. These are capital's "disposable bodies." The other victims of capitalist violence, the workers, are assembled as the "raw materials" that are then worked upon by a variety of formations (i.e., NGOs, prisons, healthcare, the police, and religious institutions) to ensure sustained production and profits. One can easily recognize the role of police, prison guards, and parole officers in containing suffering in the criminal justice system or soldiers being deployed to "humanitarian" or "peacekeeping" missions. Among care workers—nurses, physicians, counselors, and social workers—we can see how in the capitalist context, the biomedical assembly chain coopts care into closely supervised singular tasks, checklists, and algorithms indifferent to emotional costs and benefits. These conditions are worsened especially among the growing number of care workers who are women, migrants, and people of color.

Struggles around care work in the Greek context, however, reveal our ability to exit the binary of social welfare versus neoliberal models of capitalist production around care. To reproduce ourselves with divergent forms of useful labor to feed, heal, house, garden, and love beyond the logic of monetary relations and divisions of labor. Such a process requires that we disassociate completely from NGOs or professional institutions that seek to extract from and coopt autonomous forms of life into newer models of commodifiable care. Capitalist institutions organized around care are desperate to discover new diseases to consume more of its drugs, surgical supplies, and medical interventions. These institutions work in tandem with the state to individualize and pacify a potentially militant exploited public.

Instead, as the writings from the Social Space for Health, an autonomous occupied neighborhood clinic in Athens and Healthcare Center of Zagliveri occupation in the Thessaloniki region make clear, self-care practices, prescription medications, and doctors are not inherently "bad," just as herbal remedies and alternative therapies (e.g., acupuncture) are not inherently "good."[2] It is the extent to which they're individualized and distributed to those who can't afford them

---

2   See chapter nine, "The Ongoing Process of Self-Organization of Health in Petralona."

FOR HEALTH AUTONOMY

that matters. For example, what happens to caring for those people who are unable to confront the upstream causes of disease (e.g., home foreclosures or sexual violence)? Are the services organized in a manner that is hierarchical and profit-driven? Do their practices reinforce the racism, sexism, or ableism that are root causes of so much suffering?

As detailed by the healthcare initiatives of Zagliveri described in chapter three, "Details About the End of the World," and in chapter ten, "Reflections on Social Solidarity Clinics in Crete," from the Oktana Anarchist Collective, autonomous formations must distinguish between de-hospitalization versus de-institutionalization. De-institutionalization replaces the biomedical, hierarchical, and profit-centered model of modern medicine with horizontal and noncommodified modes of care. This process is determined by the assembly of healthcare workers and community residents who work cooperatively to recuperate the physical space and resources of the hospital towards an autonomous mode of production.

Several modes of de-institutionalization are discussed below that are important to highlight:

- *The embedding of an autonomous process within a mainstream healthcare setting.* "Social Solidarity Clinics in Greece" (See Chapter 6) offers reflections about autonomy by Ilektra Bethymouti, a psychologist and participant in the group that organized the first solidarity clinic in Thessaloniki. The formation of this alternative medicine group allowed for healthcare workers and patients alike to develop approaches to "breaking the doctor-patient power relationship and the integration of holistic and integral medicine."

- *Defending clinics under threat of cuts or closures.* Several contributions to this book provide analyses of how healthcare workers mobilized in response to austerity. The healthcare center mobilization in the village of Zagliveri located in the Thessaloniki region, highlight a paradigm shift in how workers organize autonomously from traditional union structures in tandem with community residents to improve conditions for health workers and patient care.

- *Recuperating abandoned clinics with the assembly model.* As described in chapter nine, "The Ongoing Process of Self-Organization of Health in Petralona," every aspect of care—from the occupation of the clinic to its daily operations—remains under the supervision of the assembly of care workers and local residents.

- *Occupying and recuperating a nonclinical space for care work.* In Thessaloniki, the worker takeover of an owner-abandoned tile factory called Vio.Me in 2013—with support from the Social Solidarity Health Center (SHC) of Thessaloniki—allowed for the creation of a care space within the factory (see contributions by Haris Malamidis in chapter four, "Workers' Medical Center at Vio.Me Self-Managed Factory" and Marta Perez, in chapter five, "Accessing the Greek Healthcare System").

Care Work Within an Anticapitalist Horizon

Greek anarchist and autonomous milieus have delegitimized and confronted the instruments of capital that subjugate and commodify new forms of care work emerging from autonomous spaces. Everything from the language, aesthetics, and modes of organizing care work are constantly at risk of appropriation by academics, NGOs, and the state, which then sell technologies and informant knowledge to capitalist industry. Although it is unlikely that the World Bank or Partners in Health would ever adopt a horizontalist assembly structure or squat abandoned clinics, they are nevertheless active in coopting the aesthetics and relationships of such spaces, the image or experience of a horizontalist assembly, the use of deprofessionalized and low-wage community health workers, the highly efficient distribution of medical supplies and coordination of volunteer physicians, and so many other autonomous care practices.

In Greece, care work collectives are also engaged in broader anticapitalist struggles—from confronting state, mafia, and fascist violence to the so-called economic crisis with its massive foreclosures, evictions, and cuts to pensions, healthcare, and social services. The intersection of so many specific and larger-scale struggles within an anticapitalist horizon transforms the potentiality of autonomous care spaces. They expand the collective body struggling to confront the instruments of power and violence and also amplify the protagonistic role of the broader anticapitalist milieu in providing access to food (e.g., farming and fishing cooperatives, social kitchens), emotional support, medical care, safe spaces, housing, etc. This process in the revolutionary struggle for health autonomy is described in depth by the Oktana collective, in their discussion of the clinic's core principles:

"A clinic provides prevention, primary healthcare, and psychosocial rehabilitation; 2) Direct action that brings to the fore the conditions of excluded populations and establishes a sustained relationship with the people concerned; 3) Defensive, promotive, and/or offensive action that is not sectorial and state mediated (union bureaucracy) but brings together health-sector workers and users; 4) De-institutionalization and de-hospitalization."

The Horizon of Care Work

The collective experiences and writings assembled here eschew the task of categorizing and defending activist or radical care spaces versus state and privately-run clinics and hospitals or Eastern versus Western medicine. Greek anarchist and autonomous milieus (among others internationally) have made such distinctions obsolete by communalizing care needs. They have expanded on how we (as care workers and users, collectives, and networks) defend what we have and reclaim what we need. However, who has the authority to determine what constitutes a need and how resources are distributed to address this need?

We start with the idea that nearly all of our healthcare needs can be addressed using preventive or primary care. In light of neoliberalism's destruction of primary care, there exists a need to expand the territory of care beyond the authority of the doctor, examining room, and prescriptions. And in doing so, there is potential to recuperate the more fundamental forms of care and mutual aid in everyday life.

These new forms could be described as "spheres" that exist in tandem with one another as a broader ecosystem of autonomous life. *For Health Autonomy* thus illuminates the radical imaginings and creation of new care spaces that allow us to build power to confront the systemic crises we face collectively. In Greece, these important care spaces show that power can be built through specific organizational structures and through regular coordination and circulation of experiences that are singular, plural, and transveral. Singular in the sense that assemblies nurture single or multiple care practices within one space. Plural in the forms of coordination and collaboration between care spaces (for medical supplies, knowledge, specialists). And finally, transversal in the practices of commoning sustained by communities that merge care work with other practices that respond to our collective needs and recuperate life autonomous from profits and the state (including housing, food, art, and safe spaces).

This multiplicity of overlapping singular, plural, and transversal forms allows care work to then intersect with other struggles to live beyond capitalist life. In the working-class neighborhood of Exarcheia in Athens, for instance, one sees how care work is in a constant state of transformation with other domains of autonomous life: housing (squatting, migrant living spaces), food (urban gardens, social kitchens, cooperatively run farmers markets), and safe spaces. At these critical junctures, the broader anticapitalist movement must collectivize and reflect on how social reproduction can channel direct confrontations with capital into possibilities for transversality. In the pages that follow, we explore the care work networks and collectives in Greece that reveal to all of us the planetary horizons of health autonomy.

ONE

ELEMENTS OF CARE WORK IN GREECE

CareNotes Collective

Understanding how social movements transition from physical or emotional distress to collectivizing around distress is fundamental to autonomous care work. Such a process is not limited to dystopian reactions against Western medicine or individualist narratives inherited from capitalist life. It's rooted in a polyvalent desire to socialize around distress, to liberate useful labor from wages, to recuperate our bodies and ecosystems in a moment where the most basic infrastructures supporting our survival—such as housing, healthcare facilities, and clean water supply—are becoming scarcities. The ability to collectively recuperate our bodies and ecosystems is dependent upon a horizon that is also able to disrupt the very instruments of class and power that reproduce our distress. Below we discuss in further detail how spaces, collectives, and analyses around disease and distress constitute some of the emerging aspects of autonomous care work in Greece and how these have emerged in opposition to, and beyond modern medicine, the state, and capitalist life.

The Crisis of the Biomedical and Electoral Models

The privatization of essential clinical services combined with the increasing demand for care by those suffering from intensifying capitalist life has led to a public health crisis in Greece. Rates of suicide, heroin addiction, HIV, and depression have escalated. These trends expose two fundamental crises at the clinical and societal level which simultaneously open new possibilities in care work.

At the clinical level, there is the inability of the biomedical model (the traditional clinical approach to diagnosis and treatment almost entirely centering biological factors) to observe, articulate, and intervene against the causes leading to the present public health crisis—austerity and migration. This is at first glance, correctly attributed to shortages in staffing and infrastructure following cuts in healthcare and social services. However, these budget cuts only expose more inherent limitations of the biomedical model to respond to larger-scale contradictions of capitalist life that manifest in so many forms of suffering.

A major inherent limitation of the biomedical model is rooted in the workflow of modern healthcare—from disease to waiting room, to doctor/patient encounter, to allocation of prescription, to consumption of pills. Commodified modes of Eastern or alternative therapies in the United States also mimic this flow—organizing suffering around the individual who, as a consumer, exchanges money with an expert healer. There is no encounter between suffering bodies in the architecture of the clinic; the doctor/healer diverts the potentiality of collectivizing around suffering to instead individualize disease with coded complaints and a prescription exchanged for a bill. Suffering = the biological = the commodifiable. There is no time to diverge from this flow or even consider alternatives to larger-scale crises such as austerity and migration.

Such a blind faith in the doctor–prescription–state-run universal healthcare structure forsakes our capacity to collectivize around suffering and reclaim the means to recuperate life as we desire. Alienation from our capacities to heal runs parallel with our inability to farm or feed ourselves due to the commodification of every facet of life. Thus, in the spirit of defending what we have and reclaiming what we need to build community, we defend universal healthcare as that desired by users and care workers, rather than politicians and CEOs; we also seek to reclaim land from mono-agriculture, abandoned buildings for housing and clinics, and so forth with principled acknowledgement of all those dispossessed in the original and ongoing histories of settler colonialism and racial capitalism.

How is the crisis of the biomedical model linked with that of the electoral? In Greece, the decades-long economic and political crisis has been met by some communities and healthcare workers not only reclaiming clinics to offer healthcare, but in the process, inspiring users and care workers to collectivize around economic and political causes of suffering. Such a desire to collectivize and politicize suffering relates to a larger-scale crisis of electoral or representational politics following the election of Syriza. This process—of collectivizing and politicizing suffering—has occurred entirely autonomous from capital while also in resistance to a self-proclaimed "progressive" state that has only escalated police violence against anarchist or migrant squats, healthcare workers, and educators resisting closures, tenants facing evictions, among other care workers and users suffering from austerity.

In the Greek context, we see three trends:

1. A revitalization of community and worker-run spaces as being crucial for the reproduction of autonomous life. This includes housing squats, care-work spaces via social clinics and recuperated hospitals, social kitchens, gardens, and safe spaces.

2. A rupture of care processes from institutionalized healthcare and emergence within spaces traditionally demarcated for noncare functions, such as factories, commercial buildings, and parks. In other words, we see social kitchens entering the plazas, squats turning into community self-defense committees against the police and mafia, or the integration of care work within a recuperated factory.

3. City, regional, and national networks of autonomous and anarchist care spaces and collectives sharing their experiences, pooling knowledge, and coordinating solidarity efforts against the sustained assault of the police, media, and state.

Liberating Care Work from Healthcare

Presently in Greece, care work has already been transferred from a profit-driven model to assemblies of care workers and community members that sustain a horizontal and participatory structure. Such assemblies abandon traditional frameworks that embrace the state, capital, institutions, and experts as mediating the collective ownership of modes of care reproduction, and instead recuperate spaces around need as it is defined emotionally, medically, and politically by care workers and users.

The possibility of shifting from healthcare to care reproduction would not be possible, however, without the transformation of identities among participants in radical care spaces. The potential to provide free healthcare services for an occupied clinic, recuperate clinics at risk of closure as a collective of healthcare workers traditionally separated by hierarchies and salaries, and collaborate with care workers not institutionally trained in care work, are some of the many ruptures of radical care work versus traditional healthcare emerging in Greece. Such outcomes are dependent on two significant and overlapping processes.

The first, and most obvious, of these processes is the deconstruction of biomedical authority and decommodification of care work provided by doctors but also nurses, therapists, social workers, and other workers. Second, the encounters within radical care spaces between healthcare workers and collective members who lack formal training in healthcare yet are indispensable to the growth of the care space. Both processes further liberate the de-institutionalization of care. However, the methodical rupture of institutionalized relations between participants of care collectives is based on broadening the understanding of care work as defined by need, as well as theoretical analysis. For instance, in Haris Malamidis' description of the Workers' Medical Center at Vio.Me Self-Managed Factory, three-member teams consisting of a doctor, a mental health specialist, and a third member potentially lacking formal training are together critical in treating "each human being as psychosomatic-social totality." This transformation from volunteer healthcare workers to care workers is further shaped with bi-monthly assemblies and a theoretical and practical training for every participant joining the Workers' Medical Center.

Decommodifying Care: From Waged Healthcare Worker to Volunteer, to Care Worker, to Deterritorialized Care Participant

Assemblies of radical care spaces mostly consist of participants with no formal training in healthcare but were core to the regular functioning of spaces. Assemblies often struggled to involve more doctors, nurses, and traditional healthcare workers with the assemblies or the upkeep of spaces. Nonetheless, the exchanges between traditional healthcare workers, nonprofessionalized participants in care spaces, and individuals receiving care are each crucial in the conception of more radical forms of care work.

The process in which peoples' identities transform from–to–between doctor–nurse to healthcare worker to care worker to deterritorialized care participant is not a linear or phasic process. It emerges out of need and articulates itself in singular or overlapping roles. For instance, the radical doctors we spoke with working in a traditional hospital unit could also participate in a social clinic assembly and fully embrace the political potentialities of both spaces. Similarly, while some participants in social clinics were dedicated to expanding access to herbal therapies in the social clinic, they would also join community self-defense collectives to confront police and mafia violence in their neighborhood when needed.

Waged Healthcare Worker

Healthcare workers are often exhausted by meeting the daily needs of their patients while also responding to worsening working conditions and gaps in care. They're channeled to address distress at an individual and acute level without collectivizing around broader injustices. This fixation on the acute confers a savior-saved relationship between the care worker and user. It is an almost militarized dynamic with hierarchical and profit-driven modes of healthcare production, and a totally pacified consumer. Nonetheless, the experiences detailed in the following pages highlight the critical role of healthcare workers in mainstream hospitals and clinics in recuperating their workplaces against closure and/or expanding access to care in social clinics and other autonomous spaces. The politicization of traditional healthcare workers is therefore crucial in resisting the devaluation of care work while also meeting with users of healthcare services and their families to collectively improve access to care.

Volunteer Healthcare Workers

Some radical care spaces rely on a network of volunteer healthcare workers (primary care physicians, dentists, specialists, therapists) that see users either in the social clinic or in their private practice. Members of CareNotes Collective were unable to meet with any volunteer physicians or nurses while in Greece. However, radical care spaces emphasized how vital these volunteers were in managing critical care needs that often required expensive diagnostic or surgical procedures. Challenges with volunteer doctors include their lack of engagement in assemblies, refusal to take on tasks perceived as inferior to their professional status (e.g., cleaning bathrooms and triaging patients), and limits to the extent they sought to politicize their work.

Care Workers

"Care workers" is an umbrella term that includes professional healthcare workers and collective participants not formally trained in healthcare, whose labor is critical in reducing suffering for themselves and users in the community, as well as sustaining the care space both materially and politically. Their unpaid labor exists within a space that has been recuperated; it has no rent or other financial obligations. Medications, herbal remedies, and equipment can be shared freely, and any forms of patronage or funding can be rejected.

Care space participants liberate care work from its commodification. Illness is liberated from being the raw material of exploited labor, with sick bodies arranged in an assembly line, besieged by pharmaceuticals or prodded by surgical devices. Care workers are no longer devalued within the realm of wage labor. The decommodification of care workers allows for more affective, communicative, user-centered, and collective models of care. It also liberates care workers to move beyond "treating" illness and distress to "preventing" such experiences through direct action. Community decisions around procuring medications occur in tandem with planning squats for evicted individuals or creating self-defense committees in response to sexual violence commited by the mafia against migrant women and women affiliated with autonomous collectives.

Some of the trained doctors and therapists who were able to dedicate time to radical care spaces contributed in their own way to the deconstruction of biomedical and profit-driven models of care into more radical conceptions of care work. For others, the desire to politicize care work was driven by the realities of a healthcare infrastructure unable to respond to a rising number of patients suffering from the violence of austerity and migration. However, the physical and emotional toll of defending mainstream clinics against austerity while remaining engaged with autonomous care spaces was an ongoing challenge.

Deterritorialized Care Participant

For some of the autonomous care spaces, there is a desire and practical need for participants to also contribute to the broader squat, collective, and neighborhood needs, such as: self-defense workshops, creating community gardens, hosting events in the community gardens in Greek, Farsi and Arabic to create community with new migrants, organizing squats with migrants, sustaining open kitchens in the plaza, or participating in large-scale actions, such as No Border camps, marches, solidarity actions for political prisoners, etc.

The capacity to flow between overt care practices to community self-defense or squatting creates an open flow of practices that either emerge from or are synergistic with an anticapitalist horizon. Such a capacity among care collectivities ruptures against the inertia imposed by certain ideological and organizational fixtures around the specialization and hierarchization of care work practices above what may be perceived as less relevant political practices, such as squatting, direct actions, etc. In the United States, collectivities that have reproduced care work within a broader noncapitalist and decolonizing horizon include the Black Panther Party community survival programs, the Young Lords and the Lincoln Hospital takeover, Up Against the Wall Motherfucker and the "bourgeois cultural event," and more recently, with Black Lives Matter and their ongoing resistance against police violence.[1]

---

1   For more on the Black Panthers and Young Lords, see: Nelson, Alondra. Body and soul: The Black Panther Party and the fight against medical discrimination. University of Minnesota Press, 2011; Miguel Melendez. *We took the streets: Fighting for Latino rights with the Young Lords.* Rutgers University Press, 2005, pp. 162–176. See the Third World Newsreel film "Garbage" (1968, 10 mins) on this action amidst the New York City garbage collectors' strike as well as the

From Clinics to Social Clinics to Social Spaces for Health to Deterritorialized Care

An important distinction emerged between the various spaces—to what extent did each de-institutionalize the power of the biomedical model and replace it with processes based on mutual aid and non-capitalist forms of care? How was the role of the physician peripheral or complementary to the peer support groups, free workshops, and social kitchens? And in Greece, we encountered some spaces that abandoned the clinic to develop a commons in which the traumas of capitalist life were collectively addressed and the patterns of a noncapitalist mode of life, including mutual aid, social kitchens, and safe spaces, were reproduced. We offer some reflections on the different types of care spaces based on the texts and conversations shared by comrades.

The Clinic

The clinic functions by individualizing emotional or physical distress, transforming complaints into charted codes that are addressed with a prescription or surgical procedure, and concluded with a financial exchange. There is little to no time or space for care workers and users to socialize around common stressors or engage in mutual aid.

Even within such a context, the Hellenic Observatory experience (chapter eight) reveals the capacity to transform flows within a mainstream hospital setting by linking users with emotional distress

---

CareNotes interview with Ben Morea, available at commonnotions.org/carenotes. The legacies of these and many other health justice politics can be found in the Movement for Black Lives platform, available at M4BL.net.

to resources and peers. For instance, users have access to various venues for group support—self-help groups, their local Hearing Voices Network, groups that support individuals planning to stop their psychotropic medications, and workshops that empower users and their family around alternative treatment strategies.

Healthcare workers simply inform users and link them with support groups, networks, and resources. Workshops on medications, coping with emotional distress, or patients' rights empower and help patients without creating additional work for staff. These experiences rupture misconceptions among healthcare workers, particularly doctors, that any intervention or "treatment" emerging within a mainstream clinic requires their expert scrutiny and is manifested with a scalpel or pill. On the contrary, the desire among users and their family to relieve suffering creates a momentum that links traditional treatments and support groups.

The Social Clinic

The social clinic continues to offer traditional modes of healthcare with physicians and other specialists to patients requiring care. However, several ruptures occur here. The first includes changes within the clinic space and workflow. The waiting room may host assemblies or workshops. In addition to facilitating the collectivization of care, there is often an anticapitalist horizon that brings together not only individuals with psychophysical complaints—such as emotional distress or diabetes—but also those encountering similarly oppressive social conditions, including unemployment, war, or homelessness.

The Vio.Me Workers' Health Center described by Cassie Thornton highlights a shift in how users interact with care providers.

The user's psychological, economic, and social context are considered in addition to the medical complaint. This encounter is described in more detail in "A Different Medicine is Possible in Our Global Economic Crisis" (chapter two):

> Every new incomer meets with three health practitioners at the same time on their first ninety-minute visit: a general physician, a psychotherapist, and a social worker or a nonhealth practitioner. There is a health card that the social worker or third member fills out, asking questions to which the patient can answer or not.
>
> The health card covers the mental, emotional, and physical health, but also is used to note the conditions of the family, home, work, food, sleep patterns, and family relations; all are considered important aspects of health. As Frosso put it, they are trying to make a hologram of every person: a three-dimensional image of health as clear as possible to the members of the Workers' Health Center as well as to the incomer.

In such spaces, all healthcare is available for free and funded by self-organized fundraisers and donations from other autonomous networks. In Athens, donated medicines and supplies were made available to a network of radical social clinics using an online cloud system that ensured their equal distribution.

The Social Space for Health

The Social Space for Health (SSH) in chapter nine describes several important elements which differentiates their space from some of the other radical care spaces: "We use the term SSH because through seminars and self-education lessons we aim to diffuse this knowledge in society. To open a discussion about one's health problem in an assembly procedure contributes to this direction." As described by members of the space, the waiting area is seen as the heart of the clinic where assemblies, film screenings, and workshops take place.

Deterritorialized Spaces of Care

When collectives launch autonomous care work practices beyond mainstream clinics and hospitals, such as with squatting or free food in public plazas, it signifies the capacity of care work to reproduce itself as a sustainer of various spheres of everyday noncapitalist life. The most well-known example of this in Greece is Exarcheia in Athens. Film screenings, social kitchens, community gardens, and safe spaces allow all residents—including Greeks and migrants—to sustain their lives unencumbered by money relations and political violence.

From Illness as Acute/Biological to Chronic/Biological to Preventive Biological/Social to the Political Act

Acute

In the traditional biomedical clinic model, this phase of care usually involves the healthcare worker addressing a single disorder. There is less attention or time for care workers or users to reflect on the systemic causes, such as homelessness or unemployment.

Although most of the Greek radical care spaces provide some degree of acute care manageable in a traditional primary care setting, the acute pathology does not dominate and organize how the space, care workers, and users organize themselves. Distinctions between "healer" and "victim" are blurred as collectives encourage all to engage as participants to organize new forms of care even while addressing acute care needs. For instance, in the text by the Social Space for Health in chapter nine, individuals affected by unemployment or diabetes participate in assemblies for mutual aid, emotional support, and exchanging information about self-care.

Chronic

This is a longitudinal, rather than acute, approach to care. It is chiefly concerned with reducing any further complications related to one's health. In addition to a heavy regimen of medications, nonpharmaceutical care strategies such as access to improved nutrition, exercise, sleep, and housing conditions are integrated in routine practice. This mode of care work typically relies on collaboration between physicians, social workers, mental health professionals, care givers, home health aides, etc.

Preventive

The lack of a preventive health approach in the biomedical model censors politicization around the economic and political factors contributing to disease and distress. It is usually less profitable than acute or chronic care services, relies on robust state resources to implement (e.g., vaccinations, sewage, and sanitation), and sheds light on how the state and capital differentially allocate resources for or against certain subgroups. A more affluent neighborhood may benefit from the creation of parks, tree plantings, and sidewalks, while its homeless residents are denied access to drinking water, bathrooms, and shelters. However, it is also an important juncture towards collectivizing many who are denied of basic resources, such as tenants unions, squatting movements, and self-defense committees against fascist violence.

Conclusion: Autonomous Life

The symbiotic relationship between radical care spaces and broader anticapitalist struggles in Greece highlight the importance of care reproduction in sustaining new possibilities of autonomous life. The liberation of nonmedical spaces (e.g., housing squats, neighborhood plazas, kitchens, community gardens) highlight some examples of how care reproduction can address both "upstream" causes of distress while deepening our social relationships around shared needs beyond the biomedical model, the state, and profits.

TWO

A DIFFERENT MEDICINE IS POSSIBLE IN OUR GLOBAL ECONOMIC CRISIS: REINVENTING HEALTHCARE IN GREECE (AND THE UNITED STATES)

Cassie Thornton

On my way to visit the Solidarity Health Center (SHC) in Thessaloniki in the winter of 2017, I passed by a woman who was selling rings on the main commercial street. Andromeda had made each of the rings by hand. I picked one out with a Drachma, the old Greek currency, placed like a gem inside of it. Most of the rings were made using a copper wire, coiled to capture and hold whatever kind of findings Andromeda chose. Often, small scraps of leather and sometimes gems were entangled in a mess of wires that happened to also cling onto one's finger.

Andromeda was an unemployed microbiologist, now selling rings on the street. She liked using copper because of its metallic property to sterilize what it touches. She told me that simply wearing a copper ring would sterilize the hand up to ninety-nine percent. Of course, this is an overstatement. I told her I was walking back from the Solidarity Clinic and she knew where it was, though she had never visited. The next day I read an article that came out in *The Guardian*, titled: "'Patients Who Should Live Are Dying': Greece's Public Health Meltdown," which focused on the spread of preventable diseases due to cuts amounting to about one-third of Greece's total public healthcare budget. Diseases were said to spread in part because overworked doctors didn't have time to wash their hands and patients were being put in dirty hospital beds.

Debt: Bringing the World Together in Crisis

In January, I visited several solidarity clinics in Greece that serve both Greeks who have been abandoned and punished by international debt markets and migrants who have nowhere else to go besides Greece due to the closing of borders to them within Europe. The solidarity clinic movement rose to prominence during the *Indignados* uprisings of 2010 and 2011, but the idea didn't tempt my imagination because it was so far from what I could imagine wanting. As a white U.S. citizen, even one without health insurance, I assumed that I would never need to stoop down to accept or desire free, community-run healthcare. I absorbed the idea that good healthcare was expensive healthcare, even if it excluded me. After spending years researching and organizing around personal debt and its effects on collective and individual psychological, behavioral, social, and emotional life, I became curious about the ways that public debts—like Greece's—work, and how people internalize and live with them.

Through my close collaboration with scholar-activist Max Haiven, I have come to understand that the crisis that we see in places like Greece or Puerto Rico (a crisis in which financialization acts as the contemporary edge of colonialism, and which contributes to the massive grinding down and obedience of the lower classes) is the same we experience in the United States. We found debt-flows that move through individual investors who speculate on and drive corrosive gentrification in American cities, and who use the profits from flipping poor, racialized people's houses to invest in hedge funds that currently hold entire states hostage with high interest loans and lawsuits. The crisis creeps, like a virus, and no nation or community is safe.

Until Trump's election, many U.S. citizens lived as if everything was okay, even if it wasn't. That has now changed. Our culture bases dignity on our ability to pay for services. It's a culture that created Trump and that also created us, and one that loads regular people with so much debt (for housing, healthcare, education, transportation, and public services) that it breeds numbness, obedience, isolation, and narcissism. The hyperindividualistic character created by the debt keeps us from the sort of radical problem-solving that emerges in states of emergency, as it has in Greece, whose crisis is not only theirs but also ours. Hearing Greek people tell me about the personal effects of the financial crisis was complex and terrible, but also, in a way, a relief for some people. I met middle-aged women who cite the financial crisis as the birth of their new lives as radicalized people within activist communities, people who found a purpose, who were becoming more than workers and consumers, who now felt powerful, connected, and interdependent. To them, there have always been problems, but after they witnessed massive unemployment, huge taxes, home foreclosures, and cuts to all public services, they were forced to deal with what had been hidden under the surface. As American anthropologist Heath Cabot explains, the other face of the crisis is solidarity.[1]

---

1   Heath Cabot and Salvatore Poier, "Solidarity and Survival in Impoverished

Not Just Free, But Also a Different Medicine

Alongside the grassroots solidarity clinics that began to appear in Thessaloniki, the city also saw the radical worker takeover of an owner-abandoned tile factory called Vio.Me in 2013.[2] The SHC responded positively to the suggestion by Vio.Me to create a health center there. A working group for a different medicine, which grew within the SHC, stepped forward to organize some aspects of the clinic that would exist in the factory. Over a few months I spoke with two members of the group, Ilektra Bethymouti and Frosso Moureli. They shared some of the group's aims with me: to move beyond providing standard medicine for free and to overcome elements that are broken in mainstream medicine. To paraphrase elements of their writing with our conversations: Current medicine separates person from environment, doctor from patient, body from psyche, and body into many parts without putting them together again.

The Workers' Health Center is animated by the same spirit of the parent Social Solidarity Health Center, challenging the hierarchy of doctor and patient relationships. The patient is referred to as "an incomer" (the Greek word for patient means weak) to empower them to become a member of the clinic, to participate actively in the matters of their health, and to connect it with the health of their community. The attempt to allow the patient/incomer to see themselves as more than a passive receiver, a child, or a potential source of profit, and to become active in self-managing their health, is a central

---

Greece: A View from the Ground," *Tropics of Meta*, July 8, 2015. Available at https://tropicsofmeta.com/2015/07/08/solidarity-and-survival-in-impoverished-greece-a-view-from-the-ground/.

2   Learn more at http://www.viome.org/.

form of health treatment. The healing begins by undoing the subordination they have experienced as a person who has been seen either as a body, or a worker, or a person—but not all three at once. In the written words of the work group for a different medicine: "we aspire to a medical science that does not simply perceive the symptom but treats it as part of the human being as a whole. Namely as a physical/psychic/social unity—like the two sides of a coin—that cannot be possibly separated." Based on these principles, The Workers' Health Center began to put into action practices that were closer to healthcare they wanted to see.

What I explain below has been carefully narrated to me by psychiatrist and psychotherapist Frosso Moureli of the SHC collective and the work group for a different medicine. In all four endeavors, we can see (in an unprecedented way) what happens when the bank is not the boss of a healthcare facility. When healthcare is taken out of the exclusive clutches of jealous "experts," medicine can become creative and can actually produce multiple forms of mutually reinforcing types of health.

Endeavors for a Different Medicine

The first endeavor was to make a reception team at the SHC, to greet incomers in new and empowering ways. The goal was to begin to erode the fearful sublimation of authority that a person goes through when they become a patient of conventional clinics. As an outsider, I imagine that when receiving free care, there is a sense that a patient must gratefully and uncritically accept what they are given. But by helping new people understand how the clinic operates, inviting them to be active and ask questions, the reception team encouraged incomers to be discerning and proactive about their own needs and interests, and also to internalize the values of the clinic (solidarity and its power) and get involved.

The second was to hold what they called "joint sessions," a meetup for physiotherapists and incomers at the Solidarity Clinic meant to put providers and receivers of care together in a new context and so erode invisible divides and hierarchies.

The third was a group meeting for people who were affected by diabetes. For ten months, anyone was welcome to come into the group to talk about the entire cycle of the disease. This group's purpose was to cocreate a safe social space to make connections between the disease and personal history, living conditions, the social environment, and personal healthcare management. The members of the group spoke about their own needs, scientific or personal, and doing so built a community of trust, care, knowledge sharing, and support. At the end of ten months, all the members had their diabetes in good control, and two had made major life changes.

The final endeavor, still under development, is something the group called an "integrative model," and this is what drew me to Greece. First explained to me by Ilektra and then Frosso, this model is based on a different idea of health, authority, care, and expertise. In this model, the new incomer meets with three health practitioners at the same time on their first ninety-minute visit: a general physician, a psychotherapist, and a social worker. There is a health card that the social worker or third member fills out, asking questions to which the patient can answer or not. The health card covers the mental, emotional, and physical health, but is also used to note the conditions of the family, home, work, food, sleep patterns, and family relations; all are considered important aspects of health. As Frosso put it, they are trying to make a hologram of every person: a three-dimensional image of health as clear as possible to the members of the Workers' Health Center as well as to the incomer.

The answers provided by the incomer are used to fill out a health card, a new type of record that the clinic is developing. It includes a family tree, which also addresses relationship quality and matters of heredity. At a follow-up meeting, the practitioners and the incomer reflect on all the physical, social, and psychological information. Here, the group helps the incomer take steps towards treatment or cure and helps them develop a plan to do so in a way where they can manage and get support for their own healing. What does the person need in order to thrive? What considerations do they need to make in terms of family, work, and money to help them feel healthy? And what I imagine to be a future question—what social movement might they join to experience the healing capacities of solidarity?

When I last spoke with Frosso, the group was working on what to do after this initial meeting. They had seen fifty incomers in this way. For me, this integrative model feels ancient, like it has always existed, and yet it is so new—just like Greece itself.

"Our" Crisis, Our Bodies

I wanted to take something back to the United States. If their crisis is also our crisis, then their work can help us, and their learning can be our learning. As a person who had never thought critically about healthcare, this idea, and all the conversations I have had because of it, made more sense to me than any other method of medicine. So much so that it made me want to be involved with a vast reimagining of healthcare. While I don't think that American doctors will volunteer en masse, and free clinics in squatted buildings wouldn't survive in the United States, there is so much we can learn about medicine itself from the care work that is being practiced at the Workers' Health Center.

During my visit to Greece, I tried to understand whether or not the work of the clinics could also be done without doctors or specialists, without training, and without certification. How much of the free clinic was about providing basic human care, compassionate attention, and a safe space to ask questions; in contrast to in-depth medical expertise using specialized tools and medicines. As I sat in the Solidarity Clinic waiting rooms, with doctors, at assemblies, and with incomers as they met with practitioners, I learned that most of the care given didn't take the form of professional expertise—it was human connection, the provision of empathy and attention within what otherwise feels like an uncaring and alienating world where the crisis is lodged in the body. Like Andromeda's copper rings that kill bacteria "ninety-nine percent of the time," I'm not proposing that we don't need expertise at all, but that we can take more collective nonexpert responsibility over our health than we do. People can help each other; they don't need medical training to provide the preventative care and problem solving that most people need to persist.

Based on this learning at the Workers' Health Center, I am striving to create a platform for collective healthcare, accountability, and solidarity that can serve anyone falling between the widening cracks of highly regulated police states, regardless of where they live. I have been inspired to do so not only by my visit to Greece, but also by my conditions and those of my friends: we have all been made itinerant and exiled from our physical communities of support by the forces of capitalism including gentrification, the gig-economy, and changing life circumstances. Denied access to quality healthcare, but also distrustful of conventional healthcare systems which are isolating, individualizing and often toxic, we need another model. For that reason, I am in the process of developing a three-person health monitoring and diagnostic system that echoes the Greek Solidarity Clinic integrative model, but that works without clinics, hierarchies, experts, or money, and that can be used across the sometimes great geographical distances that separate us from those we trust: a viral care system that functions to empower small groups of people to focus rigorously on the medical, emotional, and social health of one person at a time. The goal is to find a systematic way that we can attend to and track the health of people around us through regular conversations (in person and virtual), close observation, and good documentation. The truth is, most Americans do not have access to professional care that is robust, patient, or caring enough to earn the name "primary care." For many of us, this network could be our best attempt at primary care.

The Hologram

Currently, this project is titled *The Hologram*, which is derived from Frosso's comment as well as the solidarity network's endeavors to make health, people, and community into complex and dimensional parts of "medicine." The first trial of the project happened as part of an exhibition called *Sick Time, Sleepy Time, Crip Time: Against Capitalism's Temporal Bullying* at the Elizabeth Foundation for the Arts Project Space in New York City. If you are curious or would like to get involved in future trials, please get in touch. You can learn more about the project at feministeconomicsdepartment.com/hologram and the exhibit at projectspace-efanyc.org/sick-time.

THREE

DETAILS ABOUT THE END OF THE WORLD:

LIVING AND FIGHTING IN THE FRAME OF THE GREEK PUBLIC HEALTH SYSTEM CRISIS

Hobo

Although a great number of struggles took place in the past decade during the deep crisis of Greek capitalism, international comrades are familiar only with the more spectacular demonstrations that occurred during certain days of the general strikes.

In what follows below, I will go through a relatively unknown series of struggles that took place in the field of public health services, and more specifically, in some public healthcare centers of the Greek provinces. As a health worker myself, I was actively engaged in these struggles.

I begin by briefly explaining the structure of the Greek National Health System (NHS). There are three distinct public healthcare structures in Greece: (1) general and specialized regional and district public hospitals, in major and smaller cities respectively, are responsible for secondary care; (2) university hospitals affiliated with the medical schools provide tertiary care; (3) mixed-structure hospitals combine secondary and tertiary care. There are also primary care centers, mainly in the small towns of Greece's provinces, and rural medical/surgical services responsible for the provision of emergency and primary care services in rural areas. The latter are connected to local networks of district hospitals to which they refer patients for secondary care.[1]

The Greek NHS was introduced in 1983 by the social-democratic political party PASOK (The Panhellenic Socialist Movement), the first center-left government to emerge in Greece after the end of the 1967–1974 military junta. It was the product of social struggles in the healthcare field that emerged after the period of military rule—and was based on a serious clash of interests between the state, the private sector (mostly physician-run private clinics), and the academic establishment composed of medical schools. The result was a complicated public health system with a permanent lack of resources, doctors, and nurses, and an extensive privately-run health services sector. Within the overstretched, understaffed, and underfunded public system, the bribery of doctors, especially surgeons, is pervasive. Many receive money under the table from patients (known as the illegal private fee or "envelope") and the pharmaceutical industry.

Inadequate public health spending was one of the main factors contributing to the fiscal crisis of Greece. Healthcare workers' struggles for fair salaries, social struggles for increased access to healthcare, and rampant bribery among hospital managers and doctors with regard to the procurement of medical supplies and treatments were

---

1   There were also the outpatients' units of workers of private sector or some semi-public organizations like the Public Power Corporation (DEH in Greek), some of which accepted emergencies, while most only nonurgent cases. The vast majority of them belong to the Social Security Organization (IKA).

common. The close relationship between doctors and politicians with the pharmaceutical and medical supply industry led to more corruption and mismanagement. For this reason, the Troika and creditors of the Greek state have recently targeted Greece's NHS under the guise of reducing debt and fiscal mismanagement.

The government then decided to restructure the public health sector—and forced the closure of many hospitals and the elimination of approximately three hundred outpatient clinics run by the largest social insurance funds (i.e., IKA). They also introduced a fee of five euros for accessing the public health system, which had been free until the Troika.

After the Troika, patients were also covering a higher percentage of treatment costs. In the past, patients were expected to pay for roughly twenty-five percent of their treatment costs, with the exception of low-income pensioners and patients with certain illnesses classified as acute, in which case they were responsible for ten percent of the cost.

Healthcare reforms passed by the Greek government in this period also included digitalization of the drug prescription system obliging doctors to prescribe generic medications (when available) rather than costly brand name or commercial drugs, as was the practice previously. Doctors were also directed to prescribe a minimum percentage of generic drugs per month.

However, the most significant intervention was the effort to devalue the entire public healthcare system. This policy reached as far as the rural public health centers where there was a hiring freeze and retired workers were never replaced, leading to severe worker shortages. Doctors were overstretched in terms of patient load and staffing longer shifts, leading to exhaustion and burnout. Healthcare centers also routinely experienced shortages in basic medical supplies.

A Paradigm Shift in the Healthcare Struggle

The last few decades have seen many struggles around public health services in Greece. However, there was a paradigm shift in 2005 that has influenced many health workers and political subjects. This took place in a small town in the north of the country, near Thessaloniki, in the region of Zagliveri. A team of doctors (all general practitioners), nurses, midwives, paramedics, etc., staffing the local healthcare center of Zagliveri (HCZ), created a workers' assembly and resisted the established culture of "social peace" imposed by the management of HCZ. Some of them were already organized in the antiauthoritarian Greek movement. The important thing is that this assembly started to mobilize workers on topics not only affecting them directly, but also on problems that had to do with patient care.

When the management of HCZ repeatedly dismissed their demands, the assembly decided to discuss them with the local community in order to open a conversation around their medical care problems surrounding HCZ. Meetings were organized in every community within the jurisdiction of HCZ. Problems surrounding patient care were put on the table and the locals were encouraged to create commissions for health in order to participate in this common struggle. Women, usually the primary caregivers for their family's children and elders, were more cognizant of the existing medical problems. They put together a list of what the community's needs were—what kind of medical supplies, specialists, etc. After a while the state decided to take drastic measures and dismissed two doctors who were members of the assembly. This sparked a wave of mobilizations including marches and protests before hospital cash desks and regional management offices. The doctors were hired back to their posts and the struggles of the assembly have continued to grow since then.

The successes of these struggles had a widespread impact. For example, they managed to save some public health services structures from closure, to cancel the five-euro fee for clinical examination, and fees for laboratory tests imposed by the past government. But more importantly, they have inspired a new mode of social struggle among workers and small farmers across Greece, including the Aegean Islands like Ikaria, Naxos and Lesvos, or with the Schimatari healthcare center in the Voiotia area near Athens.

New Elements of Social Antagonism

Many of these struggles also took place in remote rural villages. In these regions, political mediation is often implemented by the local city hall and its representatives. The social relationships in these communities tend to be more conservative and villagers may lack experience in organizing protests. However, in these small towns medical staff may develop a closer relationship with patients than in the city hospitals. This is because of patients' frequent interaction with the same staff, which is less likely to occur in bigger hospitals.

These struggles are also spreading beyond the official syndicates or labor unions. In actuality, even though they exist on paper, these traditional public health syndicates or unions in Greece are practically nonexistent. They consist of very few members, are isolated, and have little impact on alleviating everyday problems afflicting health workers. They are completely bureaucratized and each one works in isolation from the other. This is why it was easy for a minority of workers in a health workplace to organize and struggle without any interference from the official syndicate leadership.

In contrast with the usual practice of these unions, these local workers' struggles brought together all the workers of the health center: doctors, nurses, midwives, cleaners, etc. That is, all the workers willing to struggle came together.

There is an important element here: these struggles *carry the class war inside the workplace*. In the center of the conflicts of interest between private (pharmaceutical, business) and public (patients, healthcare workers), we (who want a living wage) don't recognize our colleagues who cooperate with the pharmaceutical industry, or those who ask for or accept payoffs from patients.

These struggles often don't create organizations or groups that are legal in structure, such as the existing unions. They try to rupture the traditional hierarchical relationship between doctors and other healthcare staff and patients. They emphasize that patients and generally the users of public health services have to be responsible for the self-management of their health and have to also struggle for the resources and means to do that. This is not just an ideological struggle; it is a practice of everyday life.

Importantly, these struggles are not just a "shot in the air" (a common phrase that Greek political commentators often use to denounce unions demanding industrial action.)[2] They hope to achieve many things, are utilizing a variety of tactics, and importantly, are still going on.

---

2   Calls for industrial action by unions in Greece only come from the majority of a management council of the union, and do not typically include decisions from their rank-and-file members. For this reason, when we speak about "general strikes" in Greece, it implies a greater degree of self-activity and social antagonism amongst workers than what the unions themselves inspire.

FOUR

WORKERS' MEDICAL CENTER AT VIO.ME SELF-MANAGED FACTORY: EXCEEDING THE RADICAL BOUNDARIES

Haris Malamidis

Social Solidarity Clinics and Pharmacies

Resistance and solidarity practices across social and political movements is not new to our times of crisis, nor is it surprising that these practices flourish in periods of social and political turmoil. It is rather remarkable, though, when they move beyond the previously established boundaries of radical political spaces and repertoires of contention. The Workers' Medical Center on the premises of the occupied factory of Vio.Me in Thessaloniki, Greece is one such example.

The economic crisis that erupted in 2008 shook the foundations of the financial market. Although the word "crisis" denotes a sudden moment of instability and a rapid change of the status quo, in Greece this has been transformed into a protracted period of austerity. The gradual impoverishment of large sectors of the population has been met with an increase of soup kitchens, barter clubs, social centers, and other solidarity structures.[1] Among them, Greece has experienced the growth of a number of informal Social Solidarity Clinics and Pharmacies (SSCPs).[2]

SSCPs are self-organized, voluntary collectives which provide free medicine and primary healthcare services to those who are excluded from the national healthcare system, while at the same time these spaces denounce the dissolution of the healthcare system by the continuous austerity measures imposed by the Greek government, EU, ECB, and IMF. A few SSCPs had already been established before the economic crisis. The SSCP in Rethimno, Crete, for example started its operation in 2008 in order to treat undocumented migrants who are unable to access public healthcare. Nonetheless, the budget cuts imposed on the health sector, and specifically the exclusion of around one-third of the country's population from the health system in 2011,[3] was the decisive point which set in motion the vast increase of SSCPs.[4]

---

1   Theodoros Rakopoulos, "Resonance of Solidarity: Meanings of a Local Concept in Anti-austerity Greece," *Journal of Modern Greek Studies* 32, no.1 (2014): 95–119.

2   Although the term Social Solidarity Clinics and Pharmacies is widely used in order to describe the aforementioned organizations, it should be stated that there is not a precise translation in English. The phrase is sometimes translated as "Social Clinics of Solidarity," or "Solidarity Social Medical Centers." Additionally, many social clinics have been also established by municipal and state authorities as well as by NGOs. These social clinics are different in many regards from the SSCPs, primarily in that they are staffed by paid personnel (see Haris Malamidis, "Social Clinics in Greece and the Welfare Provision," September 30, 2016, available at secondwelfare. it.) Therefore, we also use the word informally when characterizing SSCPs.

3   Charlie Cooper, "Tough austerity measures in Greece leave nearly a million people with no access to healthcare, leading to soaring infant mortality, HIV infection and suicide," *Independent*, February 21, 2014. Available at https://www. independent.co.uk/news/world/europe/tough-austerity-measures-in-greece-leave-nearly-a-million-people-with-no-access-to-healthcare-9142274.html.

4   It is estimated that around forty SSCPs currently operate in Greece. See Sofia Adam and Dimitra-Dora Teloni, *Social Clinics in Crisis-ridden Greece: The Experi-*

SSCPs coordinate themselves through a mailing list and an annual conference regarding the distribution of medicines and their involvement in common activist actions. They are organized horizontally and follow collective decision-making procedures. The volunteers of the SSCPs have established assemblies to act as their ultimate decision-making instruments. However, the SSCPs do not constitute a unified body. They are autonomous entities with different starting points and goals. Taking into consideration that SSCPs were founded to address the exclusion of many Greeks from the national health system, once the government partially rectified this issue in 2016, a great debate sparked within and among SSCPs regarding their potential dissolution. The Workers' Medical Center at Vio.Me factory presents a different story.

The Workers' Medical Center

The Workers' Medical Center started its operation in December 2015 on the premises of the occupied, self-managed factory of Vio.Me in Thessaloniki.[5] However, its story starts six months earlier. At that time, the factory workers approached the group Alternative Medicine, which operates at Thessaloniki's SSCP, to inquire about the creation of a clinic inside the factory in order to meet the Workers' medical needs.[6] Since the SSCP's operating guidelines included a clause

---

ence of Healthcare Services When the National Healthcare System Retreats, (Athens: Observatory of Economic and Social Developments, Labor Institute, Greek General Confederation of Labor, 2015).

5   For a detailed account regarding Vio.Me, see Haris Malamidis, "Reducing Hierarchies for Improved Equality in the Workplace? The Case of the Worker Cooperative Vio.Me, Greece," Master's Thesis, University of Gothenburg, 2014.

6   The group Alternative Medicine (or "other medicine" in direct translation from

prohibiting the development of clinic branches in order to avoid the imposition of hierarchies, volunteers created a working group to explore the possibility of opening a new clinic. After six months of discussions, the group of Vio.Me workers and SSCP volunteers decided to establish a new clinic, one completely autonomous from both Thessaloniki's SSCP and Vio.Me. This new clinic challenges the idea of ownership and most importantly, it questions the foundations of healthcare provision as we know it.

By treating the human being as a psychosomatic-social totality, the Workers' Medical Center provides primary healthcare services with a holistic approach. In particular, the Workers' Medical Center tries to change two fundamental aspects: first, who provides the healthcare services; and second, how these services are provided. Regarding the first issue, the conventional doctor-patient model is rejected. Instead, the new clinic adopts a holistic approach in which the former patient is treated as an "incoming" person and the doctor is replaced by the medical team. The fifteen-member medical team is comprised of three-member groups, which always consist of a general doctor-pathologist, a "psy" member (meaning psychologist, psychotherapist, or sociologist) and another member who can either be medical personnel (e.g., a nurse, orthopedist, or dentist) or not.

These changes have radical implications for practical implementations even within the context of SSCPs. Although it gives priority to the workers of Vio.Me and the workers and residents of the surrounding industrial area, the Workers' Medical Center welcomes clusters

Greek to English) employs a holistic approach to medicine and deals with the relation of patients with the SSCP as well as the doctor-patient relation.

of the broader population who do not suffer from any observable illness, as well as members of self-managed workers collectives and cooperatives operating in the city of Thessaloniki. In this way, the new clinic sets in practical terms the medical concept of prevention. The potential of incorporating nonmedical staff in the medical group sparks anew the debate regarding the role of doctors' expertise within the treatment of mental and physical health.

Once the potential incoming person books an appointment through the reception team, the medical group will interview them and create their health card.[7] As an interviewee informed me, this first consultation is considered extremely important and therefore might last up to two hours. After the health card is completed by the medical group, the general doctor examines the incoming person, consults the medical group regarding next steps, and if needed, with the help of the reception team, either calls or directs the patient to a collaborating specialist.

Coming to the second aspect of how health services are being provided, there are two elements that underline the distinctly radical character of Workers' Medical Center. The first deals with the potential incorporation of nonmedical staff into the medical group and the second lies in the way that the health card is created. Regarding the first issue, just like the majority of SSCPs, every member of the Workers' Medical Center on the medical and reception teams is obliged to undergo both a theory-based and practical training period. Additionally, apart from the general assembly of the Workers'

---

7   The people involved in the reception team and the medical team compose the total personnel of the Workers' Medical Center.

Medical Center, which takes place every fifteen days, there is also the assembly of the medical team every two to three weeks to discuss medical incidents. These two assemblies enable the interaction of the medical staff with nonmedical staff, as well as the coordination between the medical and the reception team.

The creation of the health card is another part of the radical character of the center's approach to healthcare, since the Vio.Me workers contributed to drafting the health card's contents. The health card seeks information on one's standard medical history with dental and muscular system medical background, one's psy background, and one's occupational background. This not only distinguishes the Workers' Medical Center from other SSCPs but positions it even further from the usual radical boundaries of various alternative approaches to medicine.

The Workers' Medical Center's unique, subversive approach to healthcare poses some difficulties. The provision of services to everyone that might be interested, together with the time-intensive nature of visits to the center, places restrictions on the number of people that the clinic can realistically serve. However, as an interviewee replied: "We believe that the Workers' Medical Center is not going to be an SSCP which serves 1,000 or 2,000 incidents per year but one hundred or two hundred. This is because we want to emphasize the way [that the services are being provided]." Although it had received some funding from Thessaloniki's SSCP, the expenses of the Workers' Medical Center are quite low. This lies with the fact that the clinic is situated in a squatted factory and although it has the necessary medical equipment, costly services such as a dental clinic or pharmacy—which are provided in other SSCPs—are still not available. However, the double-membership of Workers' Medical

Center doctors at Thessaloniki's SSCP, together with the existence of an external solidarity network of private doctors and doctors working in hospitals, enables the clinic to meet the needs of its participants.

Conclusion

For all their differences, Social Solidarity Clinics and Pharmacies constitute an important node of resistance in the landscape of solidarity structures in crisis-ridden Greece. Not only have they managed to provide services previously provided by the welfare state alone, they have also created a space where every member has an equal say on decision-making regardless of their social status. Moving forward, in the words of an interviewee the Workers' Medical Center at Vio.Me factory "is an open experiment [. . .] which poses as the core issue under investigation the content of health care and medicine within the community." As the same interviewee continued: "Every member of the Workers' Medical Center, both the ones working on the public health system and the ones occupied in the private sector, have understood that there is a way to implement this type of health treatment neither in the market nor in the state context." The connection between the debate regarding health treatment with the struggle against austerity have led the Workers' Medical Center to pose new questions and dilemmas that move beyond the already radical boundaries of alternative medicine and self-management. What remains is to find the answers.

FIVE

ACCESSING THE GREEK HEALTHCARE SYSTEM:
WHAT ABOUT THE RIGHT TO HEALTH?

Marta Perez

We have been speaking constantly about health and all of its constituent elements during our second trip to Greece. Our contact with the Greek health system has been intimate, and we feel the need to share what we have been able to experience and learn. When we talk about the health system in Greece, we have to address common misperceptions. The most obvious is that of the Troika, which claims that because healthcare is a public system operating in a southern European country it is intrinsically inefficient. But there are also misperceptions about the fall of the health system being due to the Troika cuts without disclosing how the public health system existed before the 2008 crisis.

To get an idea of how people accessed the public health system before and after the cuts, we spoke with several people in Thessaloniki who work in the public and private health system and also participate in the Social

Clinic of Solidarity (in Greek, the acronym is KIA). We also met with migrants who were stranded in military camps or in apartments in the city after the closure of the borders and accompanied them to hospitals and health centers. In addition to helping readers learn more about the Greek health system, we hope the following will be useful for readers who have to confront the numerous obstacles to accessing health centers every day.

Without an Entry Point

"Look, the biggest problem is that people cannot access the system. It is mounted in a way that expels people. Before [the measures of the Troika], it was a system that used the resources very poorly. It lost a lot of time and resulted in a high cost in health. But at least people found a way to access it. Now, they cannot get to the doctor they need," Basilis, a doctor in one of the big hospitals in Thessaloniki and a participant in the KIA, told us.

"They do not reach the doctor because there is no common entry point to the system." This is how it was explained to us by a group of health workers. The system has not been developed for coordination between hospitals and the very few health centers and family doctors. Thus, since its inception in 1983, referrals for a test or a specialist are done by sending people to the emergency room or by calling a friend. All professionals have a network of contacts of their own to whom they can refer their patients. Without such personal contacts, the user must fend for themselves by making their own appointments or reschedule with their doctor to advance their care.

Welcome to Greece!

"Welcome to Greece!" It was Basilis's response to our surprised faces at his explanation about how healthcare works. Karrar, a migrant friend, had used the same words that morning when we accompanied him from window to window in his attempt to get an x-ray he had been scheduled for. He went from one doctor to another for several months, then to various NGOs, realizing that he needed this x-ray after being told to do so by several professionals, none of whom were able to secure a date.

"Welcome to Greece" could well describe the chaotic health system because chaos and disorganization reigned in the country long before, and ever since, the global financial crisis of 2008. It also works to justify the intervention of the Troika and other actors whose intention is to help: to receive donations of expired medicines or to feel that they speak to you "as if here, in Thessaloniki, people were dying in the streets." These are two of the experiences that Frosso, another participant of the KIA, explained to us, and how she understood the colonizing gaze imposed by the EU's economic policies.

Let's not forget that the one who welcomed us in that ironic way was Basilis, a doctor who insists that the way the system is set up leads to an enormous amount of time and resources being wasted without serving individuals needing treatment. One of the most important obstacles encountered since 2008 are the Troika's brutal cuts, which have widened the inefficient expenditure of resources and excluded more and more people from the system.

Saving Who You Can

If the path within the Greek health system was complicated before, it is now even more difficult. Since 2008, the measures imposed by the Troika led to a reduction in state spending on medicines (from 4.37 billion in 2010 to 2.88 billion in 2012 and 2 billion in 2014), repayments (5 euros for each medical consultation), and an increase in the cost of medicines. As a result of delays in payments received from the state, pharmacies often do not buy many medicines. The budget allocated for hospitals was cut by 26 percent between 2009 and 2011. Resources for mental health were cut by 20 percent between 2010 and 2011, and by 55 percent between 2011 and 2012. The cuts have also resulted in waiting periods for specialists that can take a year and a half for an initial visit.[1] The dissolution of an incipient system of primary care in 2014, hospital closings, and the dismissals of health professionals were all undertaken to comply with the second memorandum,[2] curtailing any possibility of developing a public system that is now being surpassed by the private sector in growth.[3]

"It is a system in which people have to find a way to what they need, because the system is not going to facilitate it," explained Basilis. In this way, the responsibility to ensure appointments and follow-ups

---

1   Alexander Kentikelenis, Marina Karanikolos, Aaron Reeves, Martin McKee, David Stuckler, "Greece's Health Crisis: From Austerity to Denialism," *The Lancet*, Vol. 383, Issue 9918, 2014: 748–753.

2   Evdokia Fourkioti, "6,500 Employee Layoffs in Greek Public Sector," *Greek Reporter*, June 17, 2014. Available at https://greece.greekreporter.com/2014/06/17/6500-employee-layoffs-in-greek-public-sector/.

3   Evgenia Tzortzi, "Increasing number of Greeks opt for private healthcare insurance," *Kathimerini* (online), March 29, 2016. Available at http://www.ekathimerini.com/207423/article/ekathimerini/business/increasing-number-of-greeks-opt-for-private-healthcare-insurance.

falls on the person's commitment to achieve them. This fact, which could be seen as something that encourages the autonomy of people, in practice deepens existing social inequalities. One's knowledge of the system, their contacts, the possibilities to press and get appointments, determine what level of attention they will receive.[4] For some groups of people, such as migrants waiting in Greece after the closure of borders, this is an almost impossible exercise.

Persistent Exclusion

The measures of the second memorandum of the Troika were accompanied by a law leading to more than a third of the Greek population being excluded from the health system: all those who had been unemployed for more than a year, who were unable to afford the payment guidelines set by the state social security, and migrants. This was the moment when the KIA was created as an autonomous self-organized institution, operating as a network of health centers and pharmacies with connections to specialists in the public and private health systems.

Since 2015, the Syriza government has taken some measures with respect to the health system. In April 2015, Greek prime minister Alexis Tsipras announced the hiring of 4,500 people in public health and the cancellation of payments for health visits, amounting

---

4   Several professionals in the health system told us informal payments in hospitals—made in order to be placed higher up on the waiting list or receive more urgent attention—has reduced since 2008 "because people do not have money to pay for that." For more on "informal payments" within the Greek health system, see Vassiliki Siantou, Kostas Athanasakis, and John Kyriopoulos, "The Greek Healthcare System," *World Hospitals and Health Services.* 45 (1), 2009: 32–34.

to five euros per consultation.[5] In the summer of 2016, more and more groups were emphasizing the right to health.

In a conversation with a group of health professionals, they explained to us that no measures have been implemented to allow the right to health to be actually exercised: the same difficulties persist in affording medications, access to healthcare professionals, and necessary tests. In the words of Basilis: "Since this summer, exclusion has no voice, it is not seen, it is not named, but it is the same as it was before these new policies. They say they have returned the right to health, but they have not done anything to make that happen, and the exclusion remains the same as before."

Lost in the System

In the summer of 2016, asylum seekers were granted access to the public health system. However, many of the people stranded in Greece remain lost in the system. How? Most do not have a Greek social security number that allows individuals to request appointments, limiting their access to care through emergency rooms only. Once there, communication with health personnel is often difficult since there are no translators in health centers. Most of the time, patients are accompanied by someone who speaks some English. The degree of trust and bond that exists between the patient and their translator determines much of what is discussed during the consultation.

---

5   "El Gobierno griego creará 4.500 puestos de trabajo en la sanidad pública," *El Diario*, April 2, 2015. Available at https://www.eldiario.es/sociedad/ministro-puestos-trabajo-sanidad-publica_0_373062982.html.

Once care is received, the patient is responsible for 100 percent of the cost of the medication since prescriptions cannot be issued to those without a social security number. Because they cannot request clinic visits, they lack access to any type of follow-up appointment apart from returning to the emergency room. Even if a number is given to migrant patients to follow up with a specialist, it is almost impossible to get an appointment if they do not speak Greek.

Migrants stranded in the military camps have access to healthcare via NGOs. However, such services operate in limited capacity, often without access to specialists or laboratory testing, adequate supplies of medicines or transportation to nearby hospitals.

This inability to navigate and access the Greek health system results in harrowing situations where migrants must wait months for an urgent visit with specialists, as described by Shirin and her son Hammudi. "They offer care that is minimal, late, and bad," explained colleagues from the Solidarity Clinic, who added that, on numerous occasions, NGOs end up being, whether they want it or not, a wall of contention as a result of migrants not reaching the public system.

Another limitation that the health system faces as a result of NGOs is that all health documents are issued by the Greek public system. Paperwork offered to asylum seekers by NGOs is inadequate, causing many to become anxious and look for alternative ways to obtain official papers within a system that is always on the verge of collapse.

Finally, the enormous turnover of professionals in most NGOs does not help either, exacerbating challenges in the coordination of care or with follow-up visits for patients. At the Sindos-Frakapor refugee camp in northern Greece, Mohamed told us that he did not trust local doctors and showed us the clinical history of his eight-month-old baby: a blue notebook with stripes where each week different doctors would make their notes.

Social Clinics and Spaces of Care

In a very different manner, this same medical history was recorded for Mohamed's daughter by care workers, professionals and, when needed, the family members, in the Worker's Clinic of the occupied Vio.Me factory. This collective construction of history is one of the key aspects that Makis, one of the workers of the factory and a participant in the clinic, emphasized regarding Vio.Me. Dimitra, a friend of both the KIA and this clinic, explained that the KIA began as an autonomous structure that wanted to take charge of the health of the people excluded from the Greek public system. Although this is what they continue to do (Karrar got his appointment for his tests through the KIA), they eventually discovered that it was not just about taking care of what the public system had left behind, but also about building social institutions. In other words, healthcare in another way: more horizontal, more involved in the lives of people, more holistic and, also, more efficient. This is how the idea of starting the Worker's Clinic with the workers of Vio.Me emerged.

Balancing this commitment to experimentation with meeting the health needs of people is always difficult, especially when the "urgent" is constantly entangled with the "important." In the KIA, this work is especially complicated given the situation of the Greek public health system as well as the immensity of the health needs of the thousands of people stranded in military camps a few kilometers from the city.[6]

The debate about how to address these needs without doing the work of the NGOs and without being manipulated by the government opens a range of questions: from how to make a collective approach to health that is not limited to treating cases in isolation, to creating and sustaining links with migrant communities, and how to avoid becoming a charity.

Austerity measures deepened the gaps that already existed in the Greek health system and created new ones. They encouraged the growth of the private sector and charge a high cost for the health of the people. In turn, these gaps have offered the possibility to build something else, to imagine and invent a new way of doing health between the constant urgency and the search for emancipation, between horizontality and the disposition of professional knowledge for the common people.

---

6 The KIA has created a group to visit and work with migrants waiting in the military camps. They have documented their first visit to one of them, Cordelia Softex, in a public a report that, at the moment, is only available in Greek. See www.kiathess.gr/gr/yliko/arthra/260-prosfugiko-episkepsi-softex.

SIX

SOCIAL SOLIDARITY CLINICS IN GREECE:

Marina Sitrin in conversation with Ilektra Bethymouti

Since 2011, people throughout Greece have been forced to fight for and self-organize their healthcare. Faced with a newly imposed payment for every doctor and hospital visit and in the context of a terrible economic crisis, people found they were no longer able get treatment or purchase medicine. Some even spoke of having to choose between food and medicine to survive. As with many other areas in Greek life, people came together in assemblies and decided to use both direct action and self-organization to survive. Some neighborhood assemblies and local communities regularly organize blockades of the cashiers in clinics so that people who need care do not have to pay. Other assemblies, generally initiated by doctors, came together to organize all-volunteer health clinics. Over sixty medical clinics emerged throughout Greece, forty-eight of which were self-organized and called solidarity clinics, the remaining twelve were organized by the church, whose internal forms of organization were less clear.

These clinics provide most of the services people need on a day-to-day basis: general medicine, obstetrics, pediatrics, dental care, psychology, psychiatry, and many other services. They also run free pharmacies, based on volunteer-run and donation-based goods and services.

I spoke with Ilektra Bethymouti, a psychologist and participant in the initial group who organized the first Solidarity Clinic in Thessaloniki, about the national assembly of Solidarity Clinics. She began by sharing the surprise that all of the assembly participants had at discovering that there were no longer thirty Solidarity Clinics in Greece, as they had all thought, but sixty, and the number seems to keep rising (in fact, by 2018, there were over 92 solidarity clinics in Greece). She also immediately raised the new challenge posed by the government, and one of the reasons for the national assembly:

> There are many things coming up—we have more clinics now, we have about fifty, this is one of the things that came out of the big assembly we just had. At the same time, they are changing the law about the health system—and the question is what are we going to do about it?
>
> According to the new law, the people who currently do not have social security are supposed to have access to the public health system—this is something new, everyone having access, but at the same time this is something that the hospitals do not seem to know and they are not helping or accepting people. At the national assembly we had last weekend, of the sixty solidarity clinics, twenty-six decided to come together and organize what we named the Observatory. We decided we must discover what is happening with the hospitals, to investigate, and see if they are accepting unemployed people and people without social security, and if not, why. There are

some criteria that they are supposed to base accepting people on, but until now there are a huge number of people who have not been able to go. The law has already been passed but it is not being complied with yet. It seems that doctors in the hospitals are not informed of this new law.

When they passed the law a few months ago a number of the Solidarity Clinics began to think together and question whether it was a good idea to continue with our Solidarity Clinics as a whole or just for immigrants. We had no idea what our identity was going to be if there was access to healthcare for people. We have all decided to continue since we do not know how the situation is going to resolve itself and that there is still need, so we must continue.

The change in the law with regard to healthcare is incredibly confusing, and intentionally so. On the one hand it is presented as a solution to the current crisis, in allegedly creating access to healthcare for all (a crisis of course made by the policies of the government). On the other hand, this new healthcare system is modeled on the German system, so it's not at all free or accessible for all services and needs. As Ilektra explained:

At the same time, they are going to give healthcare for the majority—still not for everyone—but it is going to be a healthcare system that is more expensive, more like the German system. It is going to be privatized in that each type of healthcare will have a cap, so for example if you have surgery and need four days to recuperate, but are only allowed three by the new system for financial reasons, then you only get three days of coverage or the hospital will have a deficit. Imagine—the doctor's salary could depend on these things. At the same time there is "access," they are putting a price on the services and you might not be able to get what you need. It is devious on all levels. It seems like they are offering public health, but they are taking something back. The government is fixing the prices with the hospitals and private sector. So, whatever need you have is going to have a fixed price and you cannot receive more than that, even if you need it. Some of the doctors are protesting, but the new law is really complicated. In our Solidarity Clinic, for example, we had to make new groups to study this new law to try and understand what it is and what they are going to do. It is really hard, and we had to study a lot. And still so many people don't know about it.

One of the other challenges that has arisen is around the type of care that is and will be provided. The Solidarity Clinics are creating a new vision—based in practice—of healthcare and health in general organized by medical professionals, patients, and the wider community. The vast majority use horizontal forms of organization, have regular assemblies where all can participate, and try and break down the division between the professional and the person serviced. Many do not accept any money from the state, nor do they have a relationship to the state. All money comes from nonaffiliated donations. The Solidarity Clinics are autonomous from all political groups and parties.

We believe in and want self-organization because what we are achieving with self-organization is something more than giving a service; the relationship we are organizing amongst ourselves is something new. We self-organize the Solidarity Clinics with horizontal assemblies—assemblies take place in each specialization, within the entire clinic and then nationally. This is a new experience and we want to continue with it.

What self-organization gives us is the opportunity to achieve what we call a different healthcare, a different kind of health. That is what we have achieved up until now. For example, in our clinic we have a group for alternative healthcare and we are trying to change the relationship between medical experts and those who don't know their rights or have the same expertise. We are trying to change these relationships and we are doing so in ways that are very concrete. That is to say, we are finding ways together with self-organization and this changes the idea of expert, of healthcare, of how we organize amongst doctors and with pharmaceuticals. We have so many questions that we have not answered yet, but we want to work on them together and we can. This is very different than if you have a public healthcare system only with its pros and cons.

SEVEN

UPDATES ON THE NATIONAL SOLIDARITY CLINIC ASSEMBLIES:

An interview with Ilektra Bethymouti

CareNotes (CN): In your conversation with Marina, you expressed a lot of hope for the national solidarity clinic assemblies. Since the first national assembly of solidarity clinics, have there been subsequent assemblies? If yes, what have been the important national projects or decisions the clinics are working on together?

Ilektra Bethymouti (IB): The international meetings of the clinics started in 2012 and we still meet every year. It's a way of keeping connected and informed about how every clinic operates, what the problems they're facing are, and what situations they've been involved with. We also make some decisions together about our principles, etcetera. In the last national assembly, for instance, we agreed on the publication of a text describing our position on the issues facing migrants.

CN: What are important lessons for initiating and sustaining these national assemblies against the various forms of control and violence by the state? And what are steps the clinics could take to avoid exhaustion and divisions amongst one another?

IB: We are promoting a different way of working together, using nonhierarchical decision-making strategies. Additionally, all solidarity clinics work independently from the state and the market.

CN: You also predicted that Greece would be forced into a German model of healthcare privatizing many services. Has this led to an increase in solidarity clinics?

IB: We already have this model. At the same time, although all citizens without social security coverage could access the hospitals—since Syriza was in power—we still had about forty clinics, because the health system had collapsed.

CN: How has the previous government attempted to shut down any opposition from healthcare workers facing budget cuts and worsening work conditions in the state-run clinics?

IB: I don't think it did.

CN: How has Syriza attempted to ignore, take control, or directly attack autonomous social clinics? Did Syriza among other state, religious, and capitalist institutions attempt to fund social clinics as a means of control?

IB: Some Syriza members are members of the clinic. A statute of the party asks for membership in social movements among its members. So, the conflicts somehow arise from inside the decision-making process in the assemblies. A few clinics have taken money from sponsors and others have been converted into municipal clinics. These are no longer members of our network.

CN: For our readers also living in societies suffering from austerity, what are critical elements they should consider when starting a solidarity clinic? Who should be involved? What are the theoretical or conceptual frameworks, if any, they should be mindful of? Are there any useful models of prior clinics that they should study?

IB: We haven't been able to connect to prior clinics that work in the same way. We work with horizontal decision-making procedures and open assemblies and we found out later on that we were doing *commoning*. We were seeing health as a common need and care as a common good for the community.

CN: And what are lessons for sustaining such autonomous clinics locally?

IB: Our local community turned out to be really helpful and involved. A significant amount of money comes from the community. The clinics have gained social legitimation by responding to real social needs.

CN: As healthcare workers—including nurses, doctors, and social workers—deal with more stressful and exhausting work schedules, how are they able to sustain their volunteering in the solidarity clinics, the assemblies, and other political projects? Has their participation reduced in the last few years in the solidarity clinics?

IB: The participation in our solidarity clinic hasn't changed. We all give some of our free time in any way we can. We have two general assemblies per month and receive the number of visitors that we can.

CN: We are now several years into the recent wave of migration and the borders have been closed, leaving more migrants stranded in Greece. What is the current attitude of healthcare workers in both state-run clinics and the solidarity clinics regarding the provision of medical care for migrants in addition to uninsured Greeks?

IB: The migrant healthcare issue is complicated at the moment, because of NGOs and other charity organizations involved in every camp. Some migrants receive medical attention through the camp and others through the hospitals. But the whole procedure depends sometimes on long decision-making processes, with many factors involved. We attend to migrants in the clinic or we connect them to the hospitals, but our work on this issue is partial and in general we attend to emergencies or patient that have been neglected care. In both hospitals and the solidarity clinic there is an attitude of solidarity towards migrants, but they are still poorly attended in many cases because of unresolved organizational matters.

CN: How have the solidarity clinics contributed to the anti-psychiatry movement, mutual aid networks, and other collective care practices?

IB: The last few years we formed a group inside the Solidarity Clinic called the "Alternative Medicine Group." It works as a self-educational group on issues like breaking doctor-patient power relations and the integration of holistic and integral medicine. We started having mixed groups of patients that consist of doctors and incoming patients, as well as joint sessions with psychologists and primary care physicians.

CN: You mentioned the Vio.Me experience. How have the solidarity clinics ruptured the traditional healthcare concept and allowed it to be transformed spatially—existing in a factory, for example—by new social networks constituted of workers, activists, migrants and healthcare professionals? Thinking of "radical care practices," is it the space, networks, and collectives that gradually create a new mode of care practice or is this care practice something a small group have already planned and pre-defined—such as the space, clinical encounter, and networks involved?

IB: The Social Clinic of Solidarity in Thessaloniki is a social movement in itself. It has links to other local social movements, like the one against privatization of the city's water and against the mines in Khalkidhiki, the occupied factory of Vio.Me, the antiracism movement, and several others. The traditional healthcare concept is changing as far as it is related to the community's real needs and their degree of involvement. Of course, a small group of people like the Alternative Medicine Group can be really helpful in this, but there is no strategy. It's an unpredictable cocreation where community, needs, movements, and strengths work together.

CN: And have the solidarity clinics introduced any other sustainable care practices that move beyond the biomedical framework? And if so, what are some examples?

IB: The idea of psychosocial attention as a way of prevention is being applied. The Workers' Clinic in Vio.Me is an example of integral medicine being applied to the clinical encounter. It begins with a multi-dimensional interview—where the health issue is considered in relation to the social, psychological and relational issues—and a multi-professional group as well as nonprofessional group are involved in joint sessions to.

CN: Reflecting on the rise and more recent decline of the solidarity clinic movement, can you say a little more about the forces causing the deterioration or decomposition of the solidarity clinics?

IB: Solidarity clinics change—this is not a surprise to us. Solidarity clinics and pharmacies functioned as autonomous collectives in Greece. They operated within the crisis, since 2011, when the effects of the crisis on the health system became obvious. These solidarity movements, involving thousands of health specialists and other volunteers, became so strong that in 2014 there were 92 solidarity clinics and pharmacies distributed throughout Greece.

Although the movement has been so strong, with a lot of involvement of the local population, there are almost no new solidarity clinics since 2014. We also know that there are fewer solidarity clinics in 2019 than in 2015. Most of them have not disappeared, but they have changed. (We don't know their exact number, as there is very limited research on solidarity clinics in the last few years).

Regarding the decline of solidarity clinics, we could hypothesize that local needs have been covered, that there are no more volunteers, or that volunteers got tired. However, it could be more complicated than that. The majority of the solidarity clinics have not acquired a legal status and largely operate in places conceded to them. Although they have achieved social recognition and legitimation, their treatment by the authorities and other actors has not always been favorable.

For example, the government tried to integrate social solidarity practices into the design of public urban health centers; in fact, some solidarity clinics became municipal clinics.

Some other municipalities, however, had not been in favor of the clinics and their demands, while the Hellenic Pharmaceutical Association demanded that the Ministry of Health close down social pharmacies. Drug Enforcement officers have even conducted a search following a false complaint about drug trafficking in these spaces.

Meanwhile, many solidarity clinics had to face eviction, such as the biggest solidarity clinic in Athens, the Metropolitan Community Clinic at Helliniko, which operated in an area privatized under the Syriza government, while the New Democracy government promoted the construction of a casino in the area (a "project" that will destroy nine acres of greenery).

There has always been an underlying division among members of the solidarity clinics in their perception of the necessity of the clinics and their future. Some members regard the clinics as a temporary solution to the crisis, while others view them as a form of commoning, as the reappropriation of a common good and its management in a way that goes beyond the crisis. The former believe that solidarity clinics should close and that the state should assume responsibility of health care. This idea has been reinforced after a 2015 reform that enabled uninsured people to have access to the public health system. The latter envisage the continuity of clinics as communing practices.

CN: Did anything specific precipitate the end of the assemblies, locally and nationally? When did those end? What are some of the reasons why they ended?

IB: The last national assembly, the Fifth Panhellenic Meeting of Solidarity Clinics, took place in Thessaloniki, in April 2016. Since then, every clinic operates on a local base, with sector assemblies and general assemblies. In that assembly the division between clinics—as well as between members of the same clinic—became obvious. Some clinics sought sponsors (which was against the agreed principles of the solidarity clinics movement); others decided to leave the umbrella of the solidarity clinics movement and form their own coalition between clinics of the same ideology; other clinics did not even show up at the meeting. Moreover, many members of the clinics where openly promoting the idea that the clinics should close down and be replaced by the state, an idea prevalent among left-wing parties.

CN: Can you explain a little more how the movements lost power under the left government?

IB: When the clinics started to operate about three million people had no social security and no entrance to public health care. This situation changed by Syrizia, and one-third of the Greek population has been included.

At the same time, members of some solidarity clinics promoted a left ideology and were either in favor of the left government or being related to the party. So, since the left government was in power, the claim for a better health system became weaker. It could be quite contradictory for them to be in the place of the opposition to the government by keeping the solidarity clinics in operation. So, it was in the years of the left government when the discussion about closing the solidarity clinics took place. Many other members did not agree, some because they view the solidarity clinics as a process of commoning; and all of them because they recognize the demolition of the health system, where there is lack of money, personnel, and exhaustive waiting lists.

CN: Finally, what is the general thinking about what the New Democracy government represents for Greece today—especially in relation to austerity?

IB: The New Democracy party came in power with promises of big changes, and their intent was evident even in their first few months in power. One of the first changes the new government made was the exclusion of the refugees and unaccompanied minor emigrants from the public health system. They've also furthered privatization and exploitation of natural resources, for instance in the land of Halkidiki, where the Canadian Eldorando Gold Corporation operates, or in the LAMBDA Development projects for the former Hellinikon airport, the nearly five-hundred acre Metropolitan Park, as well as coastal "enhancement."

This government will realize all the neoliberal reforms that could not be implemented by previous right-wing governments. The previous right-wing government of the coalition between PASOK and New Democracy (Samaras government, 2012–2015) was responsible for implementing the terms of the memorandum, with an immense attack on labour and social rights and a campaign of over taxation that has largely been responsible for the immiseration of the lower and middle classes. As a result, that government met firm popular resistance on many fronts; it lost its legitimacy very quickly and spent its last year with a slim parliamentary majority trying to hold on to power and unable to implement its program. It was ousted before its term was complete, with a victory for Syriza in January 2015.

Unfortunately, Syriza's tenure destroyed any notion that there was an alternative to austerity. On many fronts, the Syriza-led government deepened neoliberal reforms, while at best it put some of its most ambitious projects on hold. There have been some minor victories (for instance, a return of collective bargaining as well as advances in civil rights), but overall the idea that austerity could be reversed died under Syriza rule.

In line with global developments, there has also been a conservative backlash in Greece. Syriza's progressive reforms (for instance, LGBTQ and women's rights, attempts at separation between state and church, and especially the pragmatic foreign policy that led to the resolution of the Macedonia naming conflict) activated the conservative reflexes of the voters, which New Democracy, along with the mass media controlled by its oligarch allies, exploited and reinforced. These factors led to a landslide victory for New Democracy, with the new government enjoying an unprecedented legitimacy to carry out its neoliberal reform program.

There are many indications about the course its reforms will take. Many programs of privatization that were previously on hold because of resistance (e.g. water and energy companies) will surely be restarted. One of the government's first labour reforms was the elimination of the requirement of justification for layoffs of waged workers. Public spaces that were reclaimed by local societies through long struggles were simply given over to private developers (for instance, Karatasiou in Thessaloniki and Helliniko in Athens). There is simultaneously an orchestrated attack on academic freedom and the independence of public media, and rising criminalization of social movement actions.

EIGHT

SOLIDARITY BEYOND PSYCHIATRY:
DEFENDING PEOPLE'S AUTONOMY IN THE GREEK MENTAL HEALTH SYSTEM

Hellenic Observatory for Rights in the Field of Mental Health

In the last few years, legislation has been introduced in Greece with the declared intention of protecting persons with mental health problems from acts of violence and abuse. However, this has yet to be achieved in practice. Mental distress, and other mental health problems that deviate from the "norm," are attributed to a specific form of illness which, unlike other illnesses, is considered to be beyond the mental control of its bearer. Consequently, the management of mental distress is assigned by the state to systems of social control and suppression that are incompatible with notions of illness and treatment. This practice, based on the reproduction of the relevant mentality by mental health professionals and the ignorance and fear of the public, leads to mental distress being treated as something akin to a criminal offense for which the sufferer is punished through the discrediting of their speech, personality, capacities, wishes, dreams, personal and social rights, and control over their own life.

Thus, the main principles underscoring our initiatives involve ensuring the personal and social rights of all people, whether at some point in their lives they become users of psychosocial services or not. We believe the violation of these rights constitutes violence. Moreover, the existing mental health system is largely structured in a way that produces and reproduces such forms of violence, primarily through the political and existential discrediting of its users but also through specific daily practices, both in closed institutions and in the community. This violence inevitably affects the users of these services and their families, as well as employees in the respective institutions. In this sense, society as a whole is also affected, since it maintains institutionalized practices of violence, ignorance, and exclusion of its weakest members. We contend that this directly offends the ethics and culture of society as a whole. As informed and concerned citizens, we do not wish to remain observers of this situation, hoping that this will "always concern someone else."

Likewise, our aims are:

- To begin a public discussion concerning the social management of mental distress;
- To change the prevalent view regarding mental health and so-called mental disorders;
- To inform the public on matters of the rights of users of mental health services as well as those of its providers;
- To resist the logics of institutionalization and social exclusion, and the exercise of any form of violence upon users of mental health services;
- To contribute to the development of alternative forms for the social management of mental distress;

- To defend and expand the rights of persons in distress both within and outside the mental health service system;

- To promote the view that family members of persons in distress are individuals directly concerned with matters of mental distress, who deserve equal attention, support, and the inclusion of their views along with the rest of the parties involved;

- To promote the participation of users of mental health services in all levels of decision making that concern their lives.

Actions

Information Gathering Regarding Violations of Rights

Information is gathered concerning: (a) incidences of abuse of in-patients in public and private mental health facilities; (b) cases of violations of rights of users or ex-users of mental health services, of their relatives, as well as of workers in this field; (c) incidents and concerns regarding ethical issues; and, (d) gaps in the mental health service system. On the basis of the demands or complaints it receives, the Observatory acts collectively, by initiating formal complaints, or individually, by supporting the persons concerned in defending their rights. The prerequisite for undertaking action of any kind is the concerned individual's consent, active participation, and joint shaping of decisions at every stage of the action taken.

Complaint Regarding Violations of Human Rights in Private Psychiatric Facilities

In April 2008, the Observatory sent a written complaint to the Committee for the Protection of Rights of Persons with Mental

Disorders of the Greek Ministry of Health and Social Solidarity, demanding the investigation of these abuses and violations and full restitution. Although the Committee conducted a formal investigation and made recommendations, according to persons hospitalized at the facilities concerned, nothing has changed with regard to the issues that were raised. We continue to apply pressure to the Ministry and we have initiated a media campaign on this matter.

Supporting Individual Persons in Defending Their Rights
When individuals contact the Observatory with complaints regarding violations of their rights during treatment for mental health issues or when expressing one's intention to exercise their rights, the Observatory provides support by: (a) informing them of their rights and legal ways of defending them; and, (b) referring them to lawyers or other professionals who can initiate legal action on their behalf.

Operating a Public Information Office in the Psychiatric Hospital of Thessaloniki
From 2005 until 2013, volunteer members of the Observatory worked in the Public Information Office of the Psychiatric Hospital of Thessaloniki. They provided patients and their relatives with information regarding their rights and support for any relevant action they wished to undertake.

Promoting the Psychiatric Will
The psychiatric will is a document, signed in the presence of a notary or lawyer, that contains a person's decisions regarding what they will allow and what is forbidden in the course of a prospective

compulsory or voluntary psychiatric hospitalization, according to their constitutional rights to individual freedom and self-determination. The person concerned can also name specific persons as legal representatives, who take on the responsibility to ensure, using all legal means, that the person's will is respected in case of hospitalization in a psychiatric unit. The Observatory supports anyone who wishes to compose a psychiatric will by: (a) providing information on patients' rights and the psychiatric will; (b) providing a template of a psychiatric will on its website; and, (c) making referrals to legal professionals when necessary.

Support Network for Persons Wishing to Stop Psychotropic Medication

Members of the network can be mental health professionals and persons with psychiatric experience wishing to support other persons in reducing the dosage of their psychotropic drugs or maintaining their mental health without chemical means. The network does not encourage anyone to discontinue psychotropic medication but aims to support those who have already made the decision to do so, so that they achieve this through minimizing, to whatever extent possible, the possible dangers to their health from a sudden and uninformed discontinuation. In 2015, a team of mental health professionals and alternative healers was assembled to support individuals who have decided to reduce or discontinue psychotropic medication. The team has also written a Discontinuation Support Guide. In 2016, a support group for individuals in the process of reducing medication was established.

Hellenic Hearing Voices Network

The Observatory represents the Hellenic Hearing Voices Network in Thessaloniki and is a member of the International Hearing Voices Network, or Intervoice.[1] There is a self-help/support group of persons who hear voices in Thessaloniki. We also organize events and collect and translate materials regarding the specific approach to voices and unusual beliefs. Finally, people who hear voices can receive individual support in understanding and managing their voices from members of the Observatory.

Promoting Alternative Ways of Managing Mental Distress

With an aim to promoting freedom of choice, which is fundamental to the exercise of rights of users of psychiatric services, the Observatory seeks and promotes alternative modes of managing distress by: (a) producing and translating relevant information, which is made available on the Observatory's website; (b) organizing lectures, seminars, and other public events; (c) seeking, promoting, and publicizing existing alternative practices in Greece. In the last years the Observatory has organized a number of public events on topics regarding nonpathologizing understandings of, and treatments for, severe distress. It has also organized training seminars on managing hearing voices, paranoid thoughts, and the effects of trauma. There is also a support group for mental health professionals who seek to develop alternative ways of managing distress.

---

1   See https://www.haec.gr/en/aboutus/upcoming-events/voices-network; http://www.intervoiceonline.org/about-intervoice/national-networks-2/usa.

Providing Support for Setting Up and Running Self-Help Groups

Two self-help groups operate with the support of the Observatory: (1) the aforementioned Hellenic Hearing Voices Network in Thessaloniki is a self-help group for people who hear voices and/or have unusual beliefs, and has run since 2009; (b) Free Fall is a self-help group for people with diagnoses of bipolar disorder and/or extreme experiences of grief, that has run since 2012. The Observatory also supports the setting up and operation of self-help groups in other parts of Greece.

Seminars on Psychosis

These seminars are weekly meetings of a mixed group of individuals with personal experience of distress and their relatives and friends. Experiences regarding extreme mental phenomena are experientially presented and discussed, aiming to produce new knowledge on psychosis. Seminars on Psychosis have operated in Thessaloniki and Patras since 2012.

Citizens' Mental Health Zones

This is a service providing counseling and networking for people with psychosocial demands, run in collaboration with local and neighborhood citizens' initiatives. At present, three such zones operate in the Thessaloniki area.

Networking Nationally and Internationally

The Observatory collaborates with other organizations, nationally and internationally, in order to further its aims and contribute to the dissemination of alternative models and practices in the field of mental health. It is a member of the Hellenic Hearing Voices Network, Intervoice, and the European Network of (Ex-)Users and Survivors of Psychiatry (ENUSP).

NINE

THE ONGOING PROCESS OF SELF-ORGANIZATION OF HEALTH IN PETRALONA

Social Space for Health of the Neighborhood Assembly of Petralona, Koukaki, and Thissio (Athens)

From the late nineties until the early 2000s, PIKPA was a neighborhood center where immigrant families and locals from Petralona and Thissio in Athens would receive primary healthcare. In the early 2000s, PIKPA was shut down by the state. The two-story stone house remained abandoned until April 2009, when the Neighborhood Assembly of Petralona, Koukaki, and Thissio, driven by the momentum of the December 2008 revolt, decided to occupy the building to meet the needs of the neighborhood by establishing the Social Space for Health.

The Social Space for Health (SSH) is not a product of the capitalist crisis even though it emerged to manage its consequences. In our minds, even if this were not a time of social decay, there are still many reasons to create and maintain this project. We have a particular understanding of physical and mental health and recognize that social harmony with oneself and the environment thrives in a collective rather than individualistic structure. Today, we aspire to realize this experiment as a pathway to a future classless society. We believe we must build our own self-organized structures here and now, to experiment with and test self-constitution on ourselves. Our aim is to be a hub for the communication of health issues that arise in the community. We organize events, talks, and workshops that provide opportunities to deepen our analysis and contemplation, and to develop relations and trust within the neighborhood. For example, we co-organized a talk on providing care around substance abuse in the context of the crisis,discussions on medicine in crisis, health issues in the workplace, first aid and herbal medicine workshops, a stress relief workshop, as well as several film and documentary screenings.

Why "Social Space for Health" and not simply "social healthcare center"? Because we wanted to emphasize that the project is not merely a space where one can seek an appointment with a health provider. Instead we strive to create a space where the specialized knowledge of a practitioner will complement the patient and their knowledge of their own body and life. This interaction is not based on an unequal power dynamic between the two parties but is rather an attempt at a more balanced, egalitarian approach. Thus, the name of our project signifies an equal participation of health practitioners and other members. We don't assign greater value to any role; we believe that they are all intertwined. SSH is an ongoing learning process for all members and discussions are often derived from the queries we receive from everyone. We see this in cases where someone visits the space with a particular query and it is answered by another client with similar symptoms or experiences before their private consultation with a practitioner. In other cases, nonhealth practitioners obtain the ability to handle simple and specific patient requests, for example, measuring blood pressure.

Ultimately, we use the term Social Space for Health because we aim to circulate this knowledge throughout society, we are concerned with organizing our collective response to the collapse of the healthcare system and the increasing exclusion of certain populations, and because there are no white medical uniforms or sterilized walls, but a warm environment where someone can feel relaxed and discuss their problem with us. The process of constructing a different approach to health involves informing the patient to the extent that they may take an active and decisive role in their own health. To open a discussion about one's health issues in a collective fashion contributes to this goal. We do not see illness as an accursed disease that should remain enclosed within depressing hospital corridors, but as a condition that requires its own special time, space, and care. To build a space for health that also combines other social activities and groups of people (e.g. children's groups, Spanish lessons, and film screenings) creates a more immediate relationship of the patient/resident to healthcare and emphasizes care as a part of their social life rather than an interruption from it. Moreover, we use name Social Space for Health because we consider ourselves part of the society which acts from and for all of its constituent members. Consequently, any mediation by, and connection to, institutional "solidarity" agents is unthinkable and unnecessary for us.

SSH is open to all from locals and migrants, the insured and uninsured, and neighbors from Petralona or elsewhere. Just as we aspire to a health system that is available to everyone, so too have we in our self-organized space chosen to never ask for documentation or identification. We would rather rack our brains finding a way to manage demand that radically increases than impose terms and conditions that limit access to care.

A crucial reason behind our choice to not impose terms and conditions is that this project is a wager that goes beyond the initial step of tending to healthcare needs and expands to bring issues of biopolitics and the management of our bodies (in relation to those who appear as the experts on the matter, i.e. doctors) to the forefront.

The Assembly for Health

People from the Assembly for Health (a collective of health practitioners and others formed in December 2008) also participated in the local neighborhood assemblies. Thus, a parallel processing of issues such as health-as-a-right, free access to medical services, and working conditions in the medical field was initiated. Aside from intervening in medical issues and creating an accessible health space for everyone (which would not only service the poor), the main aim of the Assembly for Health was to develop the theory and practice for another kind of healthcare—one that deviates away from commercialization, oppressive, unbalanced power relations, and medicalization—and moves towards our aims to diffuse knowledge and maximize the ability of individuals to participate in decisions for their own health.

After a series of theoretical studies and practical interventions in hospitals, the next step for SSH was to squat the stone house in Ano Petralona. Housing this project in a squat was intentional. We defend this choice and juxtapose it to the authority's abandonment of PIKPA as a primary healthcare point. Housing our project in PIKPA had a double meaning from the beginning: both practically and symbolically.. The former because the equipment that was abandoned is now being used; and the latter because the local community has effectively self-organized an alternative healthcare structure to compensate for the state's closure of a primary healthcare center. Our existence and the consistency of our activity throughout these years is living proof that such a choice is possible. Naturally, we also defend this choice as a tool in our struggle with which we to respond to social needs.

In this context, the prospect of getting licensed by the state sounds to us rather like an oxymoron and a joke. The only licensing that self-organized projects require is the sense of responsibility of the people who build them and grant them their social legitimacy. SSH is housed in a squatted building and as such has always been extra-legal—not with regards to established medical criteria, but rather in relation to the statist criteria set by its language of power, which wants everything to be controlled and mediated by it. We believe it is time for us to reclaim our confidence in interpersonal dependency and move away from the concept of service as a product or commodity.

The project became a preliminary consultation space for health and was open two days a week; two hours at a time. This was the first attempt to establish a primary healthcare project in the neighborhood, which evolved from its initial form in the summer of 2011. Since then, the primary healthcare structure in the former PIKPA building has been reformed, participants have increased in number, and the project has been renamed the Social Space for Health.

The practice of recording and analyzing incoming requests for care provides a means for understanding the kind of demands the SSH has been able to respond to so far and helps us determine what additional steps can be taken to meet a higher standard of care.

Between November 2011 and the end of February 2013, SSH received hundreds of requests. The majority are for orthopedic problems, followed by requests for sociopsychological support. Many requests that seem at first to be pathological in nature have sociopsychological roots and require the appropriate treatment. This clearly stems from the intensity of economic devastation and marginalization many have faced as a result of Greece's debt crisis.

At any given moment various specialists participate in SSH, including a general internist, an otolaryngologist, a pulmonologist, an orthopedist, a psychiatrist, psychologists, pharmacists, dentists, and a dental technician. From time to time a reflexologist, neurologist, and a surgeon also participate. Through an evolving process, a sociopsychological support system has been formed which is now fully functioning. It is particularly notable that people who visited the space seeking psychological help are now equal participants in the project's assembly. The weekly assembly consists of about thirty people. SSH also hosts a group of relatives and friends of the Hearing Voices Network of Athens. Nonhealth practitioners who first encountered the project in order to seek psychological support also took part in setting up this group. We are working to set up a dental surgery in the space and are looking into getting equipment for an eye doctor to be incorporated into the program.

The program also involves herbal medicine consultation to broaden the range of solutions Western medicine has to offer. As part of an initiative for the self-management of health, an herbal medicine workshop operates where people from the local community and beyond try to mitigate their dependency on pharmaceutical companies and make their own medicines for common illnesses.

On average SSH receives four requests for medical attention per shift, with the majority of those coming from people between the ages of twenty-one and forty who reside in the neighborhood of Petrolona. A respectable number of people over sixty also visit the space, and requests come from all over the city, ranging from Keratsini to the suburb of Kifisia. This is notable, since squatting is usually less accessible to older people than younger people, keeping in mind the fact that this is not just a social health center but one that is hosted in a squatted building (squatted spaces are rather aggressively opposed by mainstream media and petty bourgeois reflexes).

We have yet to develop a systematic way to establish contact with local migrant communities. (Many migrants from Asian countries live in Kato Petralona while in Koukaki the migrant population is mostly from Balkan countries). Migrants who have visited the space do so mainly through connections established through the movement or personal relationships. The requests coming from migrants confirm their class origin as workers who find themselves in the bottom of the pyramid: mainly hepatitis (from working as rag collectors and being exposed to various infections) and orthopedic problems (which often derive from accidents in the work place).

SSH does not receive any funding and has no relation with any political party, the city of Athens, NGOs, or medical companies. We have chosen to be autonomous and self-funded. SSH puts no price on the services it provides. There is a donation box in the space that goes towards medical expenses as well as running and maintenance costs of the building. The fact that this project is far from being self-referential or isolated, but rather is part of the wider movement is evident by the solidarity expressed by workers and collectives from Greece and abroad. For example, in April 2012, a group for social solidarity of the postal workers gifted us medical equipment (cardiographs, saccharometers, and oximeters) bought with money collected from the workers themselves.

The Problem of Assimilation and Incorporation

We perceive the possibility of social clinics and other such projects getting funding by EU grants as an attempt to assimilate and incorporate social projects into the state-capitalist framework.[1] Of course, this process is not confined to EU funding but also manifests though the activities of NGOs, various media organizations, and political parties. Although the debate on this issue is ongoing within our assembly, we highlight two points concerning this issue:

First, statist gestures such as "Solidarity for All," an organization linked to the parliamentary leftist party Syriza, are an attempt to incorporate social projects so that they no longer provide a fertile ground for antisystemic voices and militant autonomy. At the same time, the state can then decide which projects will be excluded and which projects it will integrate (depending of course on the acceptance of that process by the projects themselves). And so, an artificial distinction is created that can be manipulated by the state.[2]

Secondly, if we were to pinpoint one fundamental target of the capitalist restructuring in recent years, it would be the state's shedding of its welfare obligations it had assumed as a way to pacify the intense class struggle of previous decades. Today, we call unpaid labor "voluntary work" and cover it up with the cloak of charity so that it matches the melodramatic tone of the crisis years. Our stance is that social

---

1   These grants are often administered by government institutions that channel European funding for Greek economic and social development.

2   Solidarity for All's website, solidarity4all.gr, referred to SSH as one of the social solidarity structures operating in the city without licensing. In this context, we express our position in our texts, such as one entitled "We Will Speak for Ourselves." More info can be found at https://laikisineleusipetralona.espivblogs.net/

clinics should refuse to integrate into future schemes. Our existence should be based on solidarity and not charity, active participation and not mere volunteerism.

Consequently, we have chosen to distance ourselves completely from institutions. This is not only because we don't believe that the end justifies the means, but also because the way of thought that dictates that we could cover our needs through any means offered regardless of political cost in the prevailing grim climate provides an alibi to as well as reinforces those mechanisms which at the end of the day have imposed on us the conditions for the shortages we need to cover (e.g. dismantling of the public health system, shortages of staff and infrastructure, exclusion).

We believe that any collaboration with this death machine results in feeding this vicious cycle. Accepting funding from any institutions, including local councils or companies, is a serious breach of our values. We will not become prey to future vote soliciting. Our words and actions are of value in and of themselves and form part of the movement. Our projects are not a vehicle for climbing up the political ladder or gaining high office positions, they are designed to help the people suffering under excessive economic restructuring under austerity.

Every act of legitimizing state policy by receiving funds, despite the torrent of verbal condemnation that may go with it will eventually lead to more impoverished people on the doorsteps of social clinics. At the same time their sponsors, driven by self-interest and responsible for this policy of destruction, are content knowing that some naïve persons (to put it mildly) are selflessly doing their work for them. For decades now, NGOs have been servicing the needs of those rejected by the NHS through apolitical charity (even though exclusion from health services is a deeply political act) and focusing solely on the medical and technical aspects. Any health practitioner who is exclusively concerned with tending to the huge number of demands could easily take part in such organizations resting easy on the thought of having contributed to a humanitarian cause (albeit only partly). On the other hand, those for whom there is greater meaning in resisting enslavement as a whole, in putting a stop to this production of rejects brought about by specific policies, in ending this narrative of death, are the ones who staff the autonomous social clinics.

Horizons of Autonomous Care

We would like to see more people (from the medical profession and beyond) be inspired to support primary autonomous healthcare infrastructure. Since the beginning we have aspired to see the creation of many social clinics, not as a sterile and mechanical response to the crisis even if they reject charity, but as points of struggle, as living cells of social self-organization aiming to build those material and social prerequisites for truly taking our health into our own hands. We feel enormous joy and satisfaction seeing a number of social clinics spring up both in Greece and abroad (there are clinics in Rome and Barcelona which refer to our experience) even if we differ in our core values.

We think that the struggle in the field of health must be approached within a context of communities of struggle inside the social body, in our neighborhoods and beyond. Health must become something tangible, approachable, comprehensible, something that belongs to us, something worth fighting for. We are building more opportunities for solidarity by integrating the issue of healthcare into the context of social struggles, through interventions and actions in hospitals, the circulation of experiences social struggles in SSH, and the ongoing integration of our activity into wider social struggles.

This text is a revised version of material presented at the Polytechnic School of Athens in May 2012 and an April 2013 meeting of social health centers in Thessaloniki.

TEN

REFLECTIONS ON SOCIAL SOLIDARITY CLINICS IN CRETE

Oktana Anarchist Collective

In this brief note we respond to the question of how a self-organized health clinic can be something other than a philanthropic or humanitarian initiative. Both are characterized by an uneven and dependent relationship between two roles—providers and beneficiaries. When a clinic's operation is dependent on institutional funding, it makes contingent, depoliticized responses to consequences of structural violence. In the context of the Greek crisis, cuts to healthcare are tied to increases in the racialized and gendered criminalization of HIV-positive persons, intensified discriminatory policing of the Roma population and *sans papiers* immigrants, economic dispossession, unemployment, police coercion, everyday precariousness, internalization of guilt and shame, and eruptions of neofascism. Under these circumstances, the clinic is at best a temporary fix to the healthcare gaps created by financial cuts and restructuring.

Oktana is an anarchist-communist collective, based in the Evangelismos squat in Heraklion, Crete. We envision social liberation, and act against the state and capital for the abolition of their social forms. This includes relations of command and obedience, the naturalization of self-servitude, intersectional oppression, commodity exchange, monetary relations, hierarchical division of labor, and exploitative production relations. We see the organizing of our proletarian class as a necessary condition for social revolution, including the political organizing of anarchists, therefore we participate in the Anarchist Federation (Greece), acting in both the central political scene and at the molecular level, with an internationalist perspective.

Crete is a society predominantly agrarian in character due to the ongoing close relations between rural areas and residential centers. It is an island with demographic and economic disparities mainly between the north and the south/inland part. Nearly two-thirds of its population is located on five urban and semi-urban settlements from east to west (Chania, Rethymno, Heraklion, Ierapetra, and Ag. Nikolaos). The local economy is now phasing a procedure of tertiarization, with the gradual dominance of services and seasonal work. The core of the local proletariat is found within the enormous tourist industry next to a smaller group of immigrant agrarian workers. These two groups constitute the local precarious front.

The question of how an autonomous free health care network came to be organized within Greece's solidarity movement comes from our relationship with the social health clinic–pharmacy in Heraklion (Crete); communication with members of the self-organized health structure in Exarcheia [A.D.Y.E] (VOX squat, Athens) and the Social Space for Health (PIKPA squat, Petralona, Athens); and contact with the Action Group Against Police Violence/Arbitrariness and Fascism in the Everyday (Embros Theater squat, Athens) and the Hellenic Hearing Voices Network (Athens). We also draw inspiration from the writings and actions of the following groups: The Emancipation Movement for People with Special Needs (specifically their squatting of the Center of Rehabilitation and Treatment of Children with Special Needs in Lechaina on November 4–7, 2015); the Assembly for the Circulation of Struggles (S.KY.A); the Self-organized Social Space Pasamontaña in Korydallos, Athens); the Social Space for Health, the Assembly of Nonmediated Action in Vironas, Kesariani, Pagrati and Zografou; the Initiative for a Polymorph Movement for Psychological Health; and the Social Solidarity Clinic in Ilion, Athens, which staged an intervention at the Attica Psychiatric Hospital in Dafni and Dromokaiteio Psychiatric Hospital in Haidari on December 18, 2015.

A provisional answer to the question, we reckon, reveals four issues operating in tandem. The first is specific to the clinic's organization: (1) a social solidarity clinic provides prevention, primary healthcare, and psychosocial rehabilitation. Its operation is determined through an antihierarchical and extrainstitutional process, on the basis of equal participation and horizontal decision-making, without any distinction as to race, color, origin, sexual identity, or religion. The general assembly and teams (for the self-organization, in contrast to the self-help denomination, on various health matters) are the operation's main units. The primary role of the general assembly is neither decision-making nor consensus on political positions or practice; instead, its explicit aim is to tackle the social and class hierarchies and divisions among the people involved (organizers, clinicians, patients). The negation of the dominant medicalized approach—in favor of multifactorial healthcare in which humans are treated as a biopsychosocial whole irreducible to any individual symptom and aiming at social emancipation—does not mean the negation of any specialized medical knowledge but the negation of using that knowledge for power. The teams, however, do not mirror medical specialties in their practice and orientation. The interior architecture of the clinics also does not reproduce the zoned spatial arrangement of a typical medical clinic—with reception, administration, pharmacy, etc.—which directs users' expectations and experience accordingly.

The remaining three issues are linked to a clinic's operation. This includes (2) direct action that brings to the fore the conditions of excluded populations and establishes a sustained relationship with the people concerned. Relatedly, (3) the manner in which autonomous clinics deploy both defensive postures and actions that advance social solidarities that are neither sectorial nor state-mediated, e.g., union bureaucracy, but bring together health-sector workers and users. Finally, (4) the development of health autonomy stems from the ability of solidarity clinics to de-institutionalize and de-hospitalize the established medical institutions. This is not to be confused with the neoliberal strategies of de-hospitalization via closures, privatization, and criminalization, but rather the societal reappropriation and control of state hospitals and research/manufacture centers. Considered temporally, the reclamation of state spaces enables new forms of social coordination and cooperation, and the transformation of their scope, form and content in the long term. These actions and appropriations also support acts of political disobedience in the medium term—that is, a refusal from below to pay personal debt and taxes, an act which includes the collectivization of individual risk, in order to de facto negate the implementation of the Economic Adjustment Programs (2010–present) orchestrated by the European Union/European Central Bank/ International Monetary Fund/ECM. And in the short term, these initiatives bring together a range of existing efforts of self-organized healthcare that allow for the generalization of health autonomy.

The challenges and limits to how these four issues can actually relate needs also to be considered. Counterrevolution can come from above, in the forms of repression, recuperation or mediation—e.g., the GSC's Solidarity For All program by Syriza or the collaboration with the Ministry of Health (in the case of the Metropolitan Community Clinic at Elliniko, Athens—and from below, in the form of reproduced hierarchies, divisions, and manipulations.

The second left coalition (Syriza-ANEL) promoted social solidarity/humanitarian aid after the previous coalition governments and antimemorandum demonstrations of 2010–2012. This is similar to the first left formation (PASOK) which promoted social justice and syndicalism after the post-junta right-wing government and the series of strikes in 1974–1981. In this period, it was social justice and syndicalism because it fitted to a demand-side model of capital accumulation that was at the center of Keynesianism. Today, it is social solidarity and humanitarian aid that is recuperated because it fits to a supply-side model of capitalist accumulation that is the cornerstone of neoliberalism. For the supply-side model, in contrast to the demand-side one, wages are a production cost to be reduced, not a source of demand to be increased. Relatedly, work is an individual obligation and social insurance is a conditional social burden which is covered by the individual or charity and not by guaranteed (legal) rights. Consequently, the individual–citizen is subjectivized through stress, fear, and trauma and not through parliamentary and union mediation. Both cases are a defeat of social struggle.

To work on the aforementioned four issues in tandem is to refuse both the neoliberal and neo-Keynesian imposition of work and fractured social subjectivities, and to make visible, to demonstrate the power of, and to put into practice, our own proletarian organization and solidarity.

NOTES ON CONTRIBUTORS

Ilektra Bethymouti is a psychologist and therapist who is actively involved in sociopolitical initiatives for the rights of all in the area of mental health. She is a member of the Solidarity Social Practice Clinic (www.kiathess.gr) and the Hellenic Observatory for Rights in the Field of Mental Health (http://mentalhealthhellenicobservatory. wordpress.com), in Thessaloniki, Greece.

Silvia Federici is a feminist writer, teacher, and militant. In 1972, she was cofounder of the International Feminist Collective, which launched the Wages for Housework campaign internationally. Her decades of research and political organizing accompanies a long list of publications on philosophy and feminist theory, women's history, education, culture, international politics, and more recently the worldwide struggle against capitalist globalization and for a feminist reconstruction of the commons. Her steadfast commitment to these issues resounds in her focus on autonomy in what she calls self-reproducing movements as a powerful challenge to capitalism through the construction of new social relations.

Hobo is a healthcare worker and member of the social clinic movement in Greece.

The Hellenic Observatory for Rights in the Field of Mental Health was founded in 2006 with the purpose of safeguarding the rights of persons in the mental health system and promoting alternative, non-psychiatric ways of managing mental distress. It is a network of persons involved in the mental health system—that is to say, it includes users of psychosocial services, relatives, mental health professionals and employees, and is open to anyone who shares its philosophy and aims. The Observatory is based in Thessaloniki, Greece but it accepts demands and complaints at a national level, and organizes relevant actions, usually in collaboration with other groups.

Haris Malamidis holds a PhD in Political Science and Sociology from Scuola Normale Superiore in Italy and is a postdoctoral researcher at the Hellenic Foundation for European and Foreign Policy (Athens, Greece) in the field of migration.

Oktana Anarchist Collective is an anarchist-communist collective, based in the Evangelismos squat in Heraklion, Crete. The collective envisions social liberation, and in so doing act against the state and capital for the abolition of their social forms (e.g., command/obedience relations, naturalization of self-servitude, intersectional oppression, commodity exchange, monetary relations, hierarchical division of labor, exploitative production relations). They see the organizing of our proletarian class as a necessary condition for social revolution, therefore participate in the Anarchist Federation (Greece), acting in both the central political scene and at the molecular level, with an internationalist perspective.

Marta Perez is an adjunct professor in the Department of Anthropology at Universidad Complutense de Madrid and at Duke University in Madrid. She is also involved in Madrid's social movement for universal healthcare and participates in the activist research project *Entrar Afuera*, which focuses on radical healing practices and care work in Southern Europe.

Marina Sitrin is a writer, lawyer, teacher, organizer, militant, and dreamer. She is the editor and translator *Horizontalism: Voices of Popular Power in Argentina* (AK Press, 2006); She is the author of *Everyday Revolutions: Horizontalism and Autonomy in Argentina* (Zed Books, 2012). Sitrin is coauthor of *They Can't Represent US! Reinventing Democracy from Greece to Occupy* (Verso, 2014) and *Occupying Language: The Secret Rendezvous with History and the Present* (Zucotti Park Press, 2012) with Dario Azzellini.

The Social Space for Health is based in the neighborhood assembly of Petralona, Koukaki and Thissio in Athens.

Cassie Thornton has worked primarily in the field of social practice over the past decade, engaging with the way debt affects the imagination. She works with large and small groups in the United States and abroad to orchestrate collective rituals and practices for understanding how debt and financial suffering encodes itself in our bodies and our relationships.

ABOUT CARENOTES COLLECTIVE

Intensifying inequality and violence have heightened the need to deepen our capacity to resist, offer concrete alternatives, and reproduce ourselves in the process. CareNotes Collective organizes directly on this terrain and seeks to record and amplify the experiences of those struggling for health autonomy in their own communities. Our challenge is to imagine how to expand these practices while defending our communities from the risks of cooption, state violence, and emotional trauma as well as financial domination.

ABOUT COMMON NOTIONS

Common Notions is a publishing house and programming platform that advances new formulations of liberation and living autonomy.

Our books provide timely reflections, clear critiques, and inspiring strategies that amplify movements for social justice.

By any media necessary, we seek to nourish the imagination and generalize common notions about the creation of other worlds beyond state and capital. Our publications trace a constellation of critical and visionary meditations on the organization of freedom. Inspired by various traditions of autonomism and liberation—in the U.S. and internationally, historically and emerging from contemporary movements—our publications provide resources for a collective reading of struggles past, present, and to come.

MONTHLY SUSTAINERS

These are decisive times, ripe with challenges and possibility, heartache and beautiful inspiration. More than ever, we are in need of timely reflections, clear critiques, and inspiring strategies that can help movements for social justice grow and transform society. Help us amplify those necessary words, deeds, and dreams that our liberation movements and our worlds so need.

Movements are sustained by people like you, whose fugitive words, deeds, and dreams bend against the world of domination and exploitation.

For collective imagination, dedicated practices of love and study, and organized acts of freedom.

By any media necessary.

With your love and support.

Monthly sustainers start at $5, $10 and $25.

At $10 monthly, we will mail you a copy of every new book hot off the press in heartfelt appreciation of your love and support.

At $25, we will mail you a copy of every new book hot off the press alongside special edition posters and 50% discounts on previous publications at our web store.

Join us at commonnotions.org/sustain.

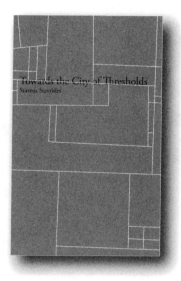

Towards the City of Thresholds
Stavros Stavrides

978-1-942173-09-0
$20.00
272 pages

Towards the City of Thresholds is a pioneering and ingenious study of new forms of socialization and uses of space—self-managed and communal—that passionately reveals cities as the sites of manifest social antagonism as well as spatialities of emancipation. Activist and architect Stavros Stavrides describes the powerful reinvention of politics and social relations stirring everywhere in our urban world and analyzes the theoretical underpinnings present in these metropolitan spaces and how they might be bridged to expand the commons.

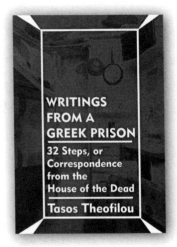

Writings from a Greek Prison
By Tasos Theofilou
Translated by Eleni Pappa
Preface by Ben Morea

978-1-942173-12-0
$15
144 Pages

Writings from a Greek Prison is a literary work of biting realism. Tasos Theofilou gives testimony on the brutality of prison life, and its centrality in contemporary capitalism, through a blur of memoir, social commentary, free verse, and a glossary of the idiom used by inmates in Greek prisons.

A political prisoner in Greece from 2012 to 2017, Theofilou's work centers on exposing the conditions of widespread exploitation and social struggle that persist in Greece as a result of the debt crisis—in prisons as well as across society.

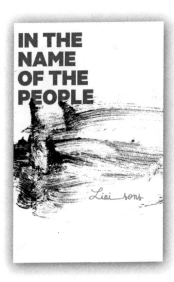

In the Name of the People
Liaisons

978-1-942173-07-6
$18.00
208 pages

The ghost of the People has returned to the world stage, claiming to be the only force capable of correcting or taking charge of the excesses of the time. *In the Name of the People* is an analysis and reflection on the global populist surge, written from the local forms it takes in the places we inhabit: the United States, Catalonia, France, Italy, Japan, Korea, Lebanon, Mexico, Quebec, Russia, and Ukraine. The upheaval and polarizations caused by populist policies around the world indicates above all the urgency to develop a series of planetary revolutionary interpretations, and to make the necessary connections in order to understand and act in the world.

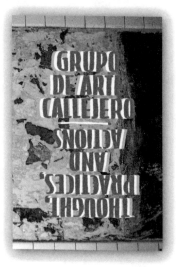

Grupo de Arte Callejero:
Thoughts, Practices, and Actions
Grupo de Arte Callejero

978-1-942173-10-6
$22.00
320 pages

Grupo de Arte Callejero: Thought, Practices, and Actions tells the pro-
found story of social militancy and art in Argentina over the last two
decades and propels it forward. For Grupo de Arte Callejero [Group
of Street Artists], militancy and art blur together in the anonymous,
collective, everyday spaces and rhythms of life. *Thought, Practices, and*
Actions offers an indispensable reflection on what was done and what
remains to be done in the social fields of art and revolution.